Contents

Thanks and acknowledgements

The author and publishers are grateful to the authors, publishers and others who have given permission for the use of copyright material identified in the text. It has not always been possible to identify the source of material used or to contact the copyright holders and in such cases the publishers would welcome information from the copyright owners.

For the extract on p. 10: adapted from 'Visible energy proves a sensual wonder' by Lynn MacRitchie, *The Financial Times,* 22 July 2000, © The Financial Times Ltd; for the extract on p. 11: from *David Hockney* by Marco Livingstone, © 1981, 1987 and 1996 Thames & Hudson Ltd, London. Reprinted by kind permission of the publisher; for the extract on p. 13: from pp. 4 and 6, *History of Art – 3rd Edition* by Marcia Pointon, published by Routledge, 1997. Reprinted by permission of T&F Informa; for the extract on p. 16: from 'Words of a Feather' by Paul Evans, published by BBC Worldwide Ltd, March 2000; for the extract on pp. 34–35: adapted from *Dublin 4* by Maeve Binchy, published by Century. Reprinted by permission of The Random House Group Ltd and Johnson & Alcock Ltd, © Maeve Binchy, DUBLIN 4, Poolbeg Press, 1981; for the extract on p. 36: from 'A Luddite's Lament' by Simon Jenkins, *The Times,* 24 January, 1998, © NI Syndication; for the extract on p. 37: from *Whit* by Iain Banks, published by Abacus. Reprinted by permission of Time Warner Book Group UK and Mic Cheetham Agency, © Iain Banks 1996; for the extract on pp. 40-41: from *Caught in the Light* by Robert Goddard, published by Bantam Press. Used by permission of The Random House Group Limited and The Peters, Fraser and Dunlop Group Limited © Robert and Vaunda Goddard; for the text on p. 62: adapted from 'A swan song for my brief brush with celebrity' by Richard Eyre, published in the *Guardian,* 23 December 2000, and the text on p. 65: adapted from 'Perfect Theatre' by Richard Eyre published in the *Observer,* 10 December 2000, © Richard Eyre; for the text on pp. 66–67: adapted from 'Joanna lessons' by Peter Kingston, published by the *Guardian,* 26 May 2000, © the Guardian; for the text on p. 72: from the cover of *Food for a Future,* by Jon Wynne Tyson. Reprinted by permission of HarperCollins Publishers Ltd. © Jon Wynne Tyson, 1988; for the text on p. 73: 'The desire to know' adapted from *Asimov's Guide to Science* by Isaac Asimov. Reprinted by permission of Basic Books, a member of Perseus Books, L.L.C., and Penguin, © 1960, 1965, 1972 by Basic Books, Inc. and Penguin Books Ltd; for the extract on p. 88: adapted from 'Getting away from it all' by Alain de Botton, published in *The Sunday Times,* 2 July 2000. Reprinted by permission of PFD on behalf of Alain de Botton, © Alain de Botton; for the text on p. 89: from *Flying Visits* by Clive James, published by Jonathan Cape. Reprinted by permission of Macmillan UK Ltd, © Clive James, 1984; for the extract on p. 94: from *Hare Brain, Tortoise Mind* by Guy Claxton. Reprinted by permission of HarperCollins Publishers Ltd, © Guy Claxton, 1997.

The publishers are grateful to the following for permission to include photographs:

AA World Travel Library for p. C7 (t & b); Corbis for pp. C8 (b), C9 (t & mr); Empics for p. C9 (b); Getty Images for pp. C8 (t), C9 (ml); Imagestate for p. C6 (b); Life File Photo Library for pp. C5 (t), C7 (m); Bryan Lowry / Alamy for p. C4 (tl); Jeff Morgan / Alamy for pp. C4 (b), C6 (t); Photolibrary.com for p. C6 (m); Popperfoto.com for p. C5 (b); Punchstock / Digital Vision for p. C8 (m); Rex Features for p. C3; Worldwide Picture Library / Alamy for p. C4 (tr).

Picture research by Kevin Brown

Cover design by Dunne Scully

The recordings which accompany this book were made at Studio AVP, London.

Cambridge Certificate of Proficiency in English 4

WITH ANSWERS

Examination papers from University of Cambridge ESOL Examinations: English for Speakers of Other Languages

CAMBRIDGE UNIVERSITY PRESS
Cambridge, New York, Melbourne, Madrid, Cape Town, Singapore, São Paulo

Cambridge University Press
The Edinburgh Building, Cambridge CB2 2RU, UK

www.cambridge.org
Information on this title: www.cambridge.org/9780521611527

First published 2005
3rd printing 2006

Printed in the United Kingdom at the University Press, Cambridge

A catalogue record for this publication is available from the British Library

ISBN-13 978-0-521-61151-0 Student's Book
ISBN-10 0-521-61151-2 Student's Book

ISBN-13 978-0-521-61152-7 Student's Book with answers
ISBN-10 0-521-61152-0 Student's Book with answers

ISBN-13 978-0-521-61155-8 Cassette Set
ISBN-10 0-521-61155-5 Cassette Set

ISBN-13 978-0-521-61156-5 Audio CD Set
ISBN-10 0-521-61156-3 Audio CD Set

ISBN-13 978-0-521-61157-2 Self-study Pack
ISBN-10 0-521-61157-1 Self-study Pack

Introduction

This collection of four complete practice tests comprises past papers from the University of Cambridge ESOL Examinations Certificate of Proficiency in English (CPE) examination; students can practise these tests on their own or with the help of a teacher.

The CPE examination is part of a group of examinations developed by Cambridge ESOL called the Cambridge Main Suite. The Main Suite consists of five examinations which have similar characteristics but are designed for different levels of English language ability. Within the five levels, CPE is at Level C2 in the *Council of Europe's Common European Framework of Reference for Languages: Learning, teaching, assessment*. It has also been accredited by the Qualifications and Curriculum Authority in the UK as a Level 3 ESOL certificate in the National Qualifications Framework. The CPE examination is recognised by the majority of British universities for English language entrance requirements, and is taken by candidates in over 100 countries throughout the world. Around 75% of the candidates are 25 years of age or under, whilst around 12% are 31 years old or over.

Examination	Council of Europe Framework Level	UK National Qualifications Framework Level
CPE Certificate of Proficiency in English	C2	3
CAE Certificate in Advanced English	C1	2
FCE First Certificate in English	B2	1
PET Preliminary English Test	B1	Entry 3
KET Key English Test	A2	Entry 2

Further information

The information contained in this practice book is designed to be an overview of the exam. For a full description of all of the above exams including information about task types, testing focus and preparation, please see the relevant handbooks which can be obtained from Cambridge ESOL at the address below or from the website at: www.CambridgeESOL.org

University of Cambridge ESOL Examinations
1 Hills Road
Cambridge CB1 2EU
United Kingdom

Telephone: +44 1223 553355
Fax: +44 1223 460278
e-mail: ESOLHelpdesk@ucles.org.uk

The structure of CPE: an overview

The CPE examination consists of five papers:

Paper 1 Reading 1 hour 30 minutes
This paper consists of four parts with 40 questions, which take the form of three multiple-choice tasks and a gapped text task. Part 1 contains three short texts, Part 2 contains four short texts and Parts 3 and 4 each contain one longer text. The texts are taken from fiction, non-fiction, journals, magazines, newspapers, and promotional and informational materials. This paper is designed to test candidates' ability to understand the meaning of written English at word, phrase, sentence, paragraph and whole text level.

Paper 2 Writing 2 hours
This paper consists of two writing tasks in a range of formats (e.g. letter, report, review, article, essay, proposal). Candidates are asked to complete two tasks, writing between 300 and 350 words for each. Part 1 (Question 1) consists of one compulsory task based on instructions and a short text or texts. Part 2 (Questions 2–5) consists of one task which candidates select from a choice of four. Question 5 has a task on each of the three set texts. Candidates choose one of the tasks in Question 5, if they want to answer on a set text. Assessment is based on achievement of task, range and accuracy of vocabulary and grammatical structures, organisation and appropriacy of register and format.

Paper 3 Use of English 1 hour 30 minutes
This paper consists of five parts with 44 questions. These take the form of an open cloze, a word formation task, gapped sentences, key word transformations and two texts with comprehension questions and a summary writing task. The two texts are from different sources and represent different treatments of the same topic. This paper is designed to assess candidates' ability to demonstrate knowledge and control of the English language system by setting tasks at both text and sentence level.

Paper 4 Listening 40 minutes (approximately)
This paper consists of four parts with 28 questions, which take the form of two multiple-choice tasks, a sentence-completion task and a three-way matching task. Part 1 contains four short extracts and Parts 2 to 4 each contain one longer text. The texts are audio-recordings based on a variety of sources including interviews, discussions, lectures, conversations and documentary features. The paper is designed to assess candidates' ability to understand the meaning of spoken English, to extract information from a spoken text and to understand speakers' attitudes and opinions.

Paper 5 Speaking 19 minutes
The Speaking test consists of three parts, which take the form of an interview section, a collaborative task and individual long turns with follow-up discussion. The standard test format is two candidates and two examiners.

Grading

The overall CPE grade is based on the total score gained in all five papers. It is not necessary to achieve a satisfactory level in all five papers in order to pass the examination. Certificates are given to candidates who pass the examination with grade A, B or C. A is the highest. The minimum successful performance in order to achieve a grade C corresponds to about 60% of the total marks. D and E are failing grades. Every candidate receives a Statement of Results which includes a graphical profile of their performance in each paper and shows their relative performance in each one. Each paper is weighted to 40 marks. Therefore, the five CPE papers total 200 marks, after weighting.

For further information on grading and results, go to the website (see page 5).

Test 1

PAPER 1 READING (1 hour 30 minutes)

Part 1

For questions **1–18**, read the three texts below and decide which answer (**A**, **B**, **C** or **D**) best fits each gap.

Mark your answers **on the separate answer sheet.**

Fashion

Fashion is often seen as a modern phenomenon, entirely **(1)** .... upon nineteenth- and twentieth-century capitalism for its development. Most historians of fashion are at **(2)** .... to point out, though, that fashion, at least in the **(3)** .... of style and design, has a very long history. They often **(4)** .... the rise of the market and mercantile trade in the sixteenth and seventeenth centuries as their starting point.

As societies have developed in complexity, populations have expanded, and multiple technologies for producing an increasing variety of clothing and physical adornment have been discovered, so the meanings attached to dress have also increased in their complexity and significance. Consequently, it is difficult to say with any **(5)** .... of certainty today what any item of clothing or adornment actually means. For example, a man's suit, **(6)** .... an indicator of the most extreme uniformity, actually conveys very differing meanings in different contexts and to different people.

	A	B	C	D
1	responsible	subject	conditional	dependent
2	effort	pains	agony	trouble
3	scale	frame	sense	aspect
4	take	get	put	make
5	ratio	element	degree	shadow
6	definitely	supposedly	evidently	obviously

Writer

Newspaper reports of publishers in **(7)** .... wars over whizz-kid manuscripts have resulted in a skewed idea of what life is like for your average novelist. Down at my end of the business – i.e. not exactly topping the best-seller lists – there are two ways of making ends **(8)** .... . The wisest among us write in the evenings and have other full-time jobs that will still be there even if the book doesn't immediately get **(9)** .... up and turned into a film. Those such as myself, however, are literary odd-jobbers, **(10)** .... on a bit of teaching, the occasional workshop and articles like this. I have **(11)** .... tell of an in-house writing opportunity offered by a chocolate factory, but I've never managed to get anything like that. Somehow, though, by **(12)** .... of juggling part-time jobs and credit cards and also, more often than not, thanks to the generosity of those names you find in Acknowledgements, the novel gets written.

	A	B	C	D
7	**A** petitioning	**B** bidding	**C** tendering	**D** proffering
8	**A** join	**B** meet	**C** connect	**D** tie
9	**A** swallowed	**B** gobbled	**C** sucked	**D** snapped
10	**A** subsisting	**B** enduring	**C** abiding	**D** prevailing
11	**A** noted	**B** heard	**C** received	**D** experienced
12	**A** way	**B** attempt	**C** dint	**D** reason

Sudden Fame

The small **(13)** .... we were performing at around the country were all beginning to sell **(14)** .... and extra bouncers were having to be called in to hold back the growing legion of screaming girls. We found ourselves having to use secret entrances to the village halls and ballrooms we were playing to prevent ourselves being mobbed by fans. On the few nights a week when we were not working, we found it difficult to leave the house without being pursued through the streets by adoring followers. In a **(15)** .... of days, we had been transformed into celebrities. Our moves were monitored by our admirers and all of our needs **(16)** .... for by our management and other interested parties. Even though the shyness that had always accompanied me never quite went away, it was replaced by a strange naive over-confidence that only naturally shy people who have been thrust into similar situations can **(17)** .... to. In short, I was emotionally totally out of my **(18)** .... .

	A	B	C	D
13	**A** sites	**B** venues	**C** scenes	**D** abodes
14	**A** out	**B** up	**C** off	**D** on
15	**A** course	**B** question	**C** spell	**D** matter
16	**A** answered	**B** catered	**C** afforded	**D** granted
17	**A** identify	**B** relate	**C** ally	**D** connect
18	**A** depth	**B** extent	**C** level	**D** reach

Part 2

You are going to read four extracts which are all concerned in some way with art. For questions **19–26**, choose the answer (**A**, **B**, **C** or **D**) which you think fits best according to the text.

Mark your answers **on the separate answer sheet**.

Kinetic Art

Rejoice – the well-nigh impossible has happened: London's austere Hayward Gallery has been transformed into a place full of wonder. And not, thankfully, by some huge-budget, mega-hyped, multi-media extravaganza, but by a charmingly idiosyncratic investigation into an almost forgotten aspect of the last 60 years. A new exhibition traces the history of kinetic art – that is art which is concerned with movement – in the twentieth century. In the process, it reveals that making artworks which either move by themselves or investigate the idea of movement in some way has been a consistent if largely unrecognised theme of some of the most fascinating creative activity of this century. And not only that – the marvellous range of paintings and drawings, documents and films on kinetic art assembled by curator Guy Brett, who has made a life-long study of the subject, are presented largely unmediated by text. Visitors, unharried by explanations, are left to have the pleasure of making connections and discoveries for themselves.

19 The writer likes the fact that the new art exhibition seems

- **A** perplexing.
- **B** colourful.
- **C** unpretentious.
- **D** unambitious.

20 Which of the following does the writer say about kinetic art?

- **A** It is stimulating social change.
- **B** It has not received the attention it deserves.
- **C** It is likely to become more popular in the future.
- **D** It has informed some better known works from the mainstream of art.

David Hockney

Hockney's work appeals to a great many people who might otherwise display little interest in art. It may be that they are attracted to it because it is figurative and, therefore, easily accessible on one level, or because the subject matter of leisure and exoticism provides an escape from the mundanities of everyday life. Perhaps it is not even the art that interests some people, but Hockney's engaging personality and the verbal wit that makes him such good copy for the newspapers. He may, in other words, be popular for the wrong reasons. But does this negate the possibility that his art has a serious sense of purpose?

In the view of some respected critics, Hockney is nothing more than an overrated minor artist. To this one can counter that Hockney might seem minor because it is unacceptable today to be so popular, rather than because his work is lacking in substance. Hockney himself is not self-deluding; he is aware of his limitations and thinks that it is beside the point to dismiss his work because it does not measure up to an abstract concept of greatness. Hockney does not claim to be a great artist and is aware that only posterity can form a final judgement on his stature.

21 In the first paragraph, the writer considers the possibility that Hockney's work

- **A** is difficult for critics to appreciate.
- **B** is not the main reason for his fame.
- **C** makes important points about human activity.
- **D** does not provide much for journalists to write about.

22 What is Hockney's own view of his work?

- **A** It is not intended to have much substance.
- **B** It bears comparison with that of earlier great artists.
- **C** Its true value will only become apparent in the future.
- **D** It does not define him as a 'great artist'.

'Window-shopping' – an art exhibition

In the last few years I have seen loads of exhibitions of contemporary art, and amongst them brilliance and mediocrity. What always bugs me, though, are shows that seem to push an underlying agenda, suggesting there is a common attitude among certain artists. Sometimes it works; we really are made aware of new trends running through apparently unrelated work. More often, though, we are alerted to a dubious angle or a forced concept. This led me, as a curator, to attempt a show which stands as an antithesis to this.

Together with seven artists I took over a space in an empty warehouse. 'Window-shopping' was intended as a collection of individual artworks that related to each other purely through the fact that they proclaimed to be art. Sam Cole's *knitted cats* went barmy chasing each other round on a toy train track. In contrast Matthew Crawley's *turning on a video camera, opening it up and poking around in there until it breaks* flickered, flashed and disappeared on the monitor in the corner. These works certainly didn't fit into the 'an exhibition exploring the theme of …' category, and wouldn't usually be seen together in the same show, but why not? They did not impede each other and actually, I hope, through their contrast, gave something to each other. OK, so I haven't made any grandiose statements about the nature of contemporary art practice, but there probably aren't any to be made about what is basically an individual activity in which artists set their own parameters.

23 What was the writer making a statement against in the show called 'Window-shopping'?

- **A** a current tendency in some exhibitions
- **B** the poor standard of some exhibitions
- **C** the cosy insularity of some artists
- **D** the political message of some artists

24 What point does the writer make about art in the second paragraph?

- **A** Artistic goals are fundamentally elusive.
- **B** It is impossible to reflect reality in art.
- **C** The human spirit should not be limited by artistic rules.
- **D** Creating a work of art is a very personal experience.

Art History

People who enjoy paintings are sometimes reluctant to analyse them for fear of spoiling the richness and spontaneity of their experience. It has been suggested that some of the work done by art historians, whose concern is with theory rather than practice, ignores and indeed denies the aesthetic experience, the fundamental pleasure of looking, as well as the very special act of artistic creativity. This view is a bit like the notion that knowing the ingredients of the recipe, recognising the method of cooking and seeing the utensils employed detracts from the taste of the dish.

Acknowledging the importance of enjoying something does not, of course, preclude a thorough knowledge of the object that is arousing pleasure. It might in fact be more pleasurable if we know more about the object we are viewing. Moreover, pleasure is not a simple matter. The arousal of our senses – and how we recognise and register it – is itself open to interrogation. It is also historically located. Why we like particular characteristics of certain sorts of objects at any one time is not simply the result of our genes or our own particular personalities but is determined by values promoted within the society of which we are a part. So, while no one seeks to underestimate the importance of sensuous and instinctive responses to art objects, the notion that the sensuous is undermined by the intellectual is a legacy from a period in the past which promoted art as an alternative to thought.

25 In likening art history to food, what is the writer implying?

A Only experts should give opinions on works of art.
B There is no harm in being fully informed about art history.
C Art historians cannot appreciate basic simplicity.
D There is a lot of very mundane popular art.

26 What does the writer say in the second paragraph about our reaction to a picture?

A It should be based purely on instinct.
B It is difficult to be completely objective.
C It is purely personal and may simply be wrong.
D It stems in part from the beliefs of former times.

Part 3

You are going to read a short story. Seven paragraphs have been removed from the story. Choose from the paragraphs **A–H** the one which fits each gap (**27–33**). There is one extra paragraph which you do not need to use.

Mark your answers **on the separate answer sheet**.

REMOVAL DAY

With her children now grown, widowed Susan faces leaving the family home

The van said, Susan noticed, 'Removers of Distinction', and indeed, every distinguishing feature of the house was being removed. Everything which made it particular was being wrapped in newspaper and packed in boxes by Fred the removal man, his enormous fingers like sausages tenderly handling all the breakables; and his team of helpers, not so gentle.

27

When told that they had bought this house, Robert, then five, had asked thoughtfully, 'Mum, when you buy a house, how d'you get it home?' You could miss a little boy in the physical presence of the adult he had become; Robert was here, helping, and in particular making sure she didn't let on about the piano. Francesca was here too, also helping, in her bossy way, stubbornly certain that nobody but she, the family daughter, would be careful enough over a fine instrument like a Steinway piano.

28

She could easily imagine.

Left to herself, Susan would have warned the removers about the piano before accepting the estimate. Robert had said sternly that it was their business to see the problem, and their bad luck if they didn't. The piano now stood in solitary glory in the upstairs sitting room, the best room in the house. They would leave it till last, naturally. Sitting on the bottom stair, for all the chairs were gone now, she remembered the time they had arrived.

29

They brought it up to the turn of the stairs, and down again, and cut out banister rails, and got it jammed anyway, while little Robert looked on enthralled, and young Francesca wailed, 'We can't live in a house without a piano! We can't! I'd rather die!' And of course they couldn't; not with a musical daughter destined to be a concert pianist. They had to find a way to get it in; and a way had been found.

30

Then, from the quay below the house, where fish were unloaded from the inshore boats, a little crane was borrowed, and dragged up the hill by means of the local farmer's tractor. Finally, the piano was wrapped in blankets, hooked to the crane and gently swung safely through the gaping window, while the entranced children danced with joy at the sight of it.

31

The children were increasingly too busy to come home at weekends, and Susan was no longer so mobile in the house, and puffing as she climbed the stairs. The thought of the stairs interrupted her daydream. The banister rails were still not quite parallel; they had not been put back perfectly all that time ago. She ought to have warned the removers, surely she ought. But now it was too late. Any moment now they would find it. She looked around, dazed and panic-stricken.

32

Truth to tell she was just on the edge of them. How odd that simply moving things made them matter. Chairs and cups and things, hundreds of things, that one never noticed or gave a moment's thought to while they stayed put, now they were displaced, were full of pathos, crying out to be cared about – and she would have cried, in a moment, surely she would.

33	

It was Robert who laughed first, but then they couldn't stop laughing, relieved that it was all over. All three of them, helplessly, leaning against each other, gasping for breath and laughing more. 'What's the joke, then?' asked Fred, but he merely started them off again. So that, as they went, the three of them, arm in arm down the path for the last time, the only tears she shed were tears of laughter.

A Peter, her late husband, had come home to the crisis and had resolved it. The piano had been left in the garden while the other furniture was brought in – there was much less of it then; they had been relatively young and hard up. And next day, to everyone's surprise, a builder had been engaged to take out the first floor window.

B To the children's undisguised pleasure, the piano was miraculously unharmed after its bumpy journey. As soon as the going was safe, Francesca celebrated with an impromptu recital so full of happy relief that it moved her mother to tears.

C Only just then the piano appeared, lurching at the top of the stairs, with Fred backing down in front of it and one of the others behind. It tipped slightly. 'Easy does it!' cried Fred, and they carried it smoothly down the stairs and out of the front door, and put it down behind the removal van on the road.

D 'Are you all right, love?' Fred was saying. 'Mind yourself, it's just the piano to come now, and then we'll be on our way.' She moved from the bottom stair, heart beating. Robert and Francesca had both appeared, standing in the back of the hallway to watch. 'No tears then?' Fred said, conversationally.

E 'She doesn't look like she's going to cry on us,' observed Fred. 'That's something.' 'Do people cry?' Susan asked, intrigued. 'You'd be surprised,' said Fred. 'They go around merry as magpies helping out till it's all in the van, then you look round and there they are, crying in the middle of an empty room. They're fine when we get to the new place, mind. It's just seeing everything taken apart that upsets them.'

F It was a lovely house that she was leaving, an elegant four-storeyed building overlooking a tiny harbour. The years she had spent there, the years of the children growing up and leaving, hung around in the air, faintly present like agitated dust.

G However, the whole process had cost so much it was months before they could afford to have the piano professionally tuned. 'That's that,' Peter had said. 'That's there for ever.' But for ever is a long time.

H The day she was living through now was like that day filmed and run backwards – the piano had been carried in first. And it had got stuck on the stairs. For nearly two hours the team of removal men struggled manfully with it, until it seemed they would simply have to give up.

Part 4

You are going to read an extract from a magazine article. For questions **34–40**, choose the answer (**A**, **B**, **C** or **D**) which you think fits best according to the text.

Mark your answers **on the separate answer sheet.**

Love them, fear them, worship them; human culture has always had a lot to say about birds. But what does that say about us? Paul Evans reports

There's a bump, bump, bump coming from the greenhouse as a little brown shuttlecock bounces against the glass. It turns out to be a wren: an ominous bird, a bird of portent, augury and divination. Is it spelling out some sort of message from a world at the very edges of my imagination? Or is it just a poor bird stuck in a greenhouse?

Depending on your point of view, both could be true. Wrens have been flitting through the undergrowth of British culture ever since it began. In medieval times, a complicated system of observing the directions in which wrens flew determined the sort of luck the observer would experience. In modern times, the image of the wren remains in pictures and ceramics in many British households. Even though the early beliefs may have been watered down or even forgotten, the wren still has a perch in our consciousness and a nest in our affections. A wood without wrens is a sad, impoverished place.

This is almost certainly because there is a rich vein of folklore running through our relationships with many birds which reaches back to a time when people read the world around them differently. Where people are, necessarily, hitched more directly to natural processes for their very survival, they develop an ecological and cultural language through which the significance of other creatures is communicated. This significance is, of course, prone to cultural shifts that cause major image changes for the creatures involved. A good example of this is the red kite. During the early sixteenth century, foreign visitors to London were amazed to see red kites swooping down to take bread from the hands of children. These birds were protected and valued urban scavengers. But it was not long before they began to be seen as vermin, and as a result were soon wiped out in most areas apart from Wales. Gradually red kites began to assume a romantic personality linked to this Celtic stronghold and they have now become totemic birds of British conservation, protected again and reintroduced with a view to helping them regain their original distribution.

Our relationship with other creatures is more than cultural and goes way back to the evolution of human nature. Though the first human birdwatchers may have been acutely observant of bird behaviour because it announced approaching predators, bad weather, and the availability of food, and also offered a supernatural link to the world of their dreams, there is more to it. When we ask why birds are so important to us, we are also asking what it is to be us. Flight, song, **line 22** freedom – our fascination, envy and emulation of the avian world is surely a measure of our own identity against that of the wildness of nature. Some might dismiss these feelings as vestigial attachments, useful to us in an earlier phase of our evolution, irrelevant now. But, like the appendix and wisdom teeth, they're still very much part of us and losing them is **line 25** traumatic.

That is probably why, in recent years, birds have become the barometers of environmental change, indicators of ecological quality: the warning bells of environmentalism. Conservationists in Britain cite the endangering of 30 species, a figure that is depressing not only because it spells out the loss of feathered curiosities, but because it is a massive cultural loss too. These birds carry a huge amount of cultural baggage. For example, the skylark, turtle dove and lapwing signify spiritual **line 30** love, romantic love and magic. Anyone who has read Shelley's poems, Shakespeare's sonnets and Robert Graves's *The White Goddess* will feel more than a tug of remorse at the loss of these once commonplace birds.

Yet while the loss of these birds is lamented, the loss of others which don't figure in either literature or folklore is virtually ignored. Folklore is so important. The stories, legends and rhymes which persist through time, with their obscure origins, constant revisions and reinventions, somehow have a greater living bond with their subjects than cold, scientific terms – **line 35** a bond that is strengthened by the everyday language in which they are understood and communicated. This gives them a power to summon up feelings and attitudes from a consciousness buried under all the stuff of modern life.

Whether we watch wildlife films on TV or birdtables in the backyard, what we're doing and the excitement we get from what we see cannot adequately be captured by scientific reason. Birds are engaging in ways we still find hard to fathom, let alone articulate, and so the stories we tell about them seem like ways of interpreting what birds are telling us.

The wren in the greenhouse weaves an intricate knot, tying an imaginary thread between the here and now and a deep, distant history, holding the free end in its song and escaping into the future – a riddle that keeps me guessing.

34 In paragraph 2, the writer affirms that the wren

A has been given exaggerated importance.
B was once used as an aid to navigation.
C has lost its significance as society has become less superstitious.
D is still firmly established in collective memory.

35 What point is the writer illustrating with the example of the red kite?

A Most birds have symbolic and poetic associations.
B Human and avian life are inseparably linked.
C A society's attitude to wildlife is not fixed.
D Wildlife can threaten human society with disease.

36 The writer uses the words 'there is more to it' (line 22) to introduce the idea that

A birds enable us to analyse the nature of human existence.
B birds extend our knowledge of evolution.
C bird behaviour accurately predicts danger.
D bird behaviour is surprisingly similar to human behaviour.

37 With the reference to 'the appendix and wisdom teeth' (line 25), the writer is drawing attention to the fact that

A humans and birds have some common anatomical details.
B being separated from deep-rooted emotions can be a painful experience.
C humans cannot explain their biological inheritance.
D bonding with the natural world is as vital as maintaining physical health.

38 In what sense do some birds carry 'a huge amount of cultural baggage'? (line 30)

A They are weighed down with people's false assumptions.
B They are believed to symbolise environmental destruction.
C They figure prominently in literature through the ages.
D Their disappearance will herald the loss of cultural identity.

39 In paragraph 6, the writer draws a comparison between 'cold, scientific terms' (line 35) and

A obscure origins.
B everyday language.
C feelings and attitudes.
D stories, legends and rhymes.

40 The writer feels that the appeal of birds is

A difficult to express or explain.
B heightened by detailed study.
C understandable in a psychological context.
D enhanced by media presentation.

PAPER 2 WRITING (2 hours)

Part 1

You **must** answer this question. Write your answer in **300–350** words in an appropriate style.

---

1 A major international sports competition is about to take place and your class has been talking about the advantages of such events. During the discussion the following points were made. Your tutor has asked you to write an essay evaluating the advantages of major international sports competitions and expressing your views on the comments made during the discussion.

It's the pursuit of excellence in whatever sport you compete in.

Just an opportunity for the TV companies to fill the screens with boring sport …

… where the largest countries always win all the medals and the rest don't stand a chance …

Write your **essay**.

Part 2

Write an answer to **one** of the questions **2–5** in this part. Write your answer in **300–350** words in an appropriate style.

---

2 Your local newspaper has invited readers to send in articles entitled

'Humans and machines – who is in control?'

You decide to write an article describing the role that machines such as computers and robots play in our lives, and saying whether you think there are any long-term dangers in our dependence on machines.

Write your **article**.

3 The music magazine *High Notes* has asked readers to write a review of a concert of their favourite kind of music: for example, classical, jazz, rock or pop. You recently attended such an event. You decide to write a review of the concert focusing on what made the music so memorable.

Write your **review**.

4 You work as a journalist for the travel section of a newspaper. You have recently visited a holiday resort to find out more about it. Write a report of your visit which will be printed in the newspaper. Within your report you should include information on the hotel you stayed in, local restaurants and entertainment facilities. You should also describe the suitability of the resort as a family holiday destination.

Write your **report**.

5 Based on your reading of **one** of these books, write on **one** of the following:

(a) Anne Tyler: *The Accidental Tourist*
Your local newspaper has invited readers to contribute an article to their literature column entitled 'Sad, but funny'. Write an article about *The Accidental Tourist*, mentioning what aspects of the novel you find sad and how humour is reflected in the characters and their actions.

Write your **article**.

(b) Brian Moore: *The Colour of Blood*
You belong to a book club which has asked members to submit reports on books which portray strong leaders. You decide to write a report on *The Colour of Blood*. You should focus on the character of Cardinal Bem, and say how far you think he develops as a leader throughout the book.

Write your **report**.

(c) L.P. Hartley: *The Go-Between*
'It did not occur to me that they had treated me badly.' Write an essay for your tutor briefly describing Leo's relationship with Marian Maudsley and Ted Burgess and saying how you feel he was treated by these two adults.

Write your **essay**.

PAPER 3 USE OF ENGLISH (1 hour 30 minutes)

Part 1

For questions **1–15**, read the text below and think of the word which best fits each space. Use only **one** word in each space. There is an example at the beginning **(0)**.

Write your answers in CAPITAL LETTERS **on the separate answer sheet**.

Example: | 0 | B | E | C | O | M | E |

Getting Away From The Land

By the start of the twenty-first century, Britain had **(0)**...BECOME... a highly urbanised country, with only a small proportion of the population in touch **(1)**............ the working life of the countryside. But this has by **(2)**............ means always been the case. At the end of the nineteenth century, in excess **(3)**............ a million people were employed in agriculture, five **(4)**............ today's figure.

Even **(5)**............ , however, the total was significantly below that in most European countries, high factory wages having already tempted people to leave the countryside in favour of the industrial cities. In **(6)**............ to this, the English custom of primogeniture, by **(7)**............ land is inherited only by the eldest son, served **(8)**............ further accelerate the rural exodus.

During the war years of the 1940s, at a time **(9)**............ food was short, people seized whatever opportunities **(10)**............ were to improve their diet **(11)**............ growing their own vegetables. However, this practice soon lost **(12)**............ appeal once the war was over, as **(13)**............ other temporary expediencies, such as keeping chickens in town gardens. **(14)**............ is more, mixed arable and livestock farming, once the norm, became rare, so that even **(15)**............ people than ever were involved in agriculture.

Part 2

For questions **16–25**, read the text below. Use the word given in capitals at the end of some of the lines to form a word that fits in the space in the same line. There is an example at the beginning **(0)**.

Write your answers in CAPITAL LETTERS **on the separate answer sheet**.

Example: | **0** | E | L | E | C | T | R | I | C | A | L |

Fast Brain Waves

Over half a century ago, scientists found they could record the	
(0) ELECTRICAL signals of the brain at work. What at first appeared a random	**ELECTRIC**
hotch potch of activity became a pattern of elegant waves **(16)............**	**RHYTHM**
determined. Ever since, scientists have wondered whether	
the secrets of our thoughts, **(17)............** and even	**PERCEIVE**
(18)............ itself might be hidden in the patterns of our brain waves.	**CONSCIOUS**
The question of why we have brain waves is, **(19)............** , as hotly debated	**ARGUE**
today as it was when the patterns were discovered. But the meaning, and even	
the existence, of fast rhythms in the alert brain is highly **(20)............** .	**CONTROVERSY**
What is problematic is that you can't perceive these rhythms directly, they are so	
well hidden in the noise created by other brain activity, but many **(21)............**	**SEARCH**
now hold the **(22)............** that the significance of these brain waves should not	**CONVINCE**
be **(23)............** .	**ESTIMATE**
The latest suggestion is that the rhythms could be **(24)............** in detecting	**DECIDE**
processes going on in different regions of the brain. Some believe that these	
rhythms might even interact, and in doing so help the brain to package	
information into **(25)............** thoughts. How we bring together these related	**COHERE**
signals in the brain is a puzzle as yet unresolved.	

Part 3

For questions **26–31**, think of **one** word only which can be used appropriately in all three sentences. Here is an example **(0)**.

Example:

0 Some of the tourists are hoping to get compensation for the poor state of the hotel, and I think they have a very .... case.

There's no point in trying to wade across the river, the current is far too ....

If you're asking me which of the candidates should get the job, I'm afraid I don't have any .... views either way.

0	S	T	R	O	N	G												

Write **only** the missing word in CAPITAL LETTERS **on the separate answer sheet**.

---

26 The police were given the .... to break up gatherings of three or more people.

The study identified which fuels would have been used in electricity generation if nuclear .... had not been used.

The Chairman of the company was reluctant to hand over .... to the Board of Directors in his absence.

27 Demand for beach toys is very .... this year because of the bad summer weather.

The villagers were angered when the council spokesperson put forward a rather .... argument for closing the local school.

This tea's far too .... ; there's too much water in the pot.

28 There's no point in raising the matter again; I have no intention of changing my ....

Bettina has worked there for ten years and thinks she should have been offered a better .... in the company by now.

The airline's financial .... is healthier now than it has been for many years.

29 I think what you said yesterday .... how difficult it is to get anyone to agree on anything.

The lecturer .... his talk with a really colourful selection of slides.

It was universally agreed that the book which won the photography prize was beautifully ....

30 The party will never succeed until it manages to ease the tensions between its conservative and liberal ....

The consortium agreed that the .... for the aircraft would be made in Canada.

The hotel consists of a large block with two smaller .... on each side.

31 Sally always joins me for a .... of golf on Saturday mornings.

Our house is near the end of the postman's .... , so he doesn't get here until about 9.30.

Management are meeting with the unions for another .... of negotiations to avert the threatened strike.

Part 4

For questions **32–39**, complete the second sentence so that it has a similar meaning to the first sentence, using the word given. **Do not change the word given**. You must use between **three** and **eight** words, including the word given.

Here is an example **(0)**.

Example:

0 Do you mind if I watch you while you paint?

objection

Do you .... you while you paint?

0	have any objection to my watching

Write **only** the missing words **on the separate answer sheet**.

---

32 Anne's dedication to her work has always been exemplary.

herself

Anne .... the most exemplary way.

33 The delay is a nuisance, but I'm sure Sam can solve our problems.

come

The delay is a nuisance, but I'm sure Sam can ....
to our problems.

34 Henrik was very pleased to be selected for the team.

delight

Much .... for the team.

35 Yoshi wanted to make sure that everything was as it should be on the big day.

leave

Yoshi didn't .... on the big day.

36 The treasurer called a meeting to discuss the club's finances.

purpose

The treasurer's .... to discuss the club's finances.

37 It may seem strange, but the composer has no formal training in music.

lacks

Strange .... kind of formal training in music.

38 I've never thought of asking the hotel staff for advice about restaurants.

occurred

It has .... the hotel staff for advice about restaurants.

39 In spite of all my efforts, I couldn't persuade Soraya to come to the concert.

hard

No matter ...., I couldn't persuade Soraya to come to the concert.

Part 5

For questions **40–44**, read the following texts on language. For questions **40–43**, answer with a word or short phrase. You do not need to write complete sentences. For question **44**, write a summary according to the instructions given.

Write your answers to questions **40–44 on the separate answer sheet**.

So how did it all begin, this powerful, weird communication system of ours? Frustratingly, we do not know. Our earliest written records are around 5,000 years old, though most are more recent. Yet language must have evolved at least 50,000 years ago, and most experts propose a date 100,000 years ago. Until recently, how it all began was an unfashionable question, a playground for cranks.

Curious theories abounded. Take the views of Lord Monboddo, a Scottish aristocrat, who in 1773 published a book claiming that humans learned how to spin and weave from spiders, how to construct dams from beavers, and how to sing and speak from birds. **line 6**

As absurd claims mushroomed, the question of language origin was avoided by serious scholars. Yet scholarly disapproval did not stop speculation. One academic, in fact, has counted twenty-three 'principal theories' of language origin. Another acidly commented: 'The very fact ... that human animals are ready to engage in a great "garrulity" over the merits and demerits of essentially unprovable hypotheses, is an exciting testimony to the gap between humans and other animals.'

The origin of language is like a juicy fruit dangling just out of reach. Human beings have a natural curiosity about it seemingly built into their minds: 'Few questions in the study of human language have attracted so much attention, provoked so much controversy, or resisted so resolutely their answers as that of the origin of language,' noted a recent writer. **line 18**

40 Which phrase later in the text repeats the idea of 'Curious theories abounded.'? (line 6)

....

41 What does 'it' in line 18 refer to?

....

When we humans ever bother to think about what makes us different from all other animals, we quickly focus on language. We use it to conjure up images in our mind, whether for a solo drift in a daydream, or collectively, as we tell each other stories. Quite simply, language is our medium. In spite of this, how it evolved remains amongst the most speculative areas of investigation into human origins.

No wonder, then, that anthropologists' speculations have long been as contentious as they are imaginative. Unfortunately, of all human behaviour, the spoken word is practically invisible in the archaeological record. It doesn't manifest itself legibly in the ways that technological skills show themselves in the complexity of toolkits, or as cognitive and organisational skills imprint themselves on patterns of hunting practice. But language surely influences how these skills are used: in the standardisation of tool types or in the cohesiveness of a tribal group searching for food. But how to *know* any of these things: that's the challenge.

In a recently published book, an American linguist has offered us a state-of-the-art review of the work carried out on the origins of language. Among the patterns he sees emerging is that modern spoken language, as a tool of highly efficient communication, was the key to the success of anatomically modern humans who appeared around 150,000 years ago. It was, he argues, a simultaneous evolution of linguistic competence and a capacity for complex thought that gave us an evolutionary edge over other animals.

42 Explain the paradox in the relationship between language and humans described in paragraph 1.

....

43 Explain in your own words what **two** factors in human evolution, mentioned in paragraph 3, gave human beings an advantage over other animals.

....

44 In a paragraph of **50–70** words, summarise **in your own words as far as possible** why it has been so difficult to investigate the origins of language, as described in **both** texts. Write your summary **on the separate answer sheet**.

PAPER 4 LISTENING (40 minutes approximately)

Part 1

You will hear four different extracts. For questions **1–8**, choose the answer (**A**, **B** or **C**) which fits best according to what you hear. There are two questions for each extract.

Extract One

You hear a radio programme in which a man is talking about mountaineering.

1 The speaker feels the press coverage of mountaineering is

A untrue.
B unfair.
C unkind.

[ ] **1**

2 He suggests that people are attracted to climbing because of

A the level of regulation in the sport.
B the atmosphere amongst the participants.
C the contrast it provides with other activities.

[ ] **2**

Extract Two

You hear an educational psychologist talking at a public meeting about parents' concerns for their school-age children.

3 What is the psychologist doing when she speaks?

A describing her research with parents
B giving some reassurance to parents
C advising parents to improve their skills

[ ] **3**

4 According to the psychologist, what should parents do if their children ask for help with their homework?

A listen and offer encouragement
B suggest alternative approaches
C supply answers to a difficult task

[ ] **4**

Extract Three

You hear part of a radio interview in which a social scientist, Ricardo Benetti, talks about self-deception.

5 The interviewer says that, in Benetti's view, self-deception

A has been misunderstood as a concept.
B is a strategy employed by developed cultures.
C is a product of moral uncertainty.

6 Benetti gives the example of the watch to show that self-deception is

A essentially pointless.
B surprisingly complex.
C generally effective.

Extract Four

You hear a musician talking about classical music.

7 She refers to a documentary on the Renaissance period in order to

A emphasise her point about modern attitudes towards music.
B compare popular appreciation of music and painting.
C praise certain television programmes about music.

8 What is her attitude towards present-day musicians?

A She regrets their level of musicianship.
B She criticises their lack of imagination.
C She believes their needs are not being met.

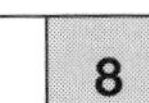

Part 2

You will hear part of a radio programme about penguins – birds which live in Antarctica.
For questions **9–17**, complete the sentences with a word or short phrase.

Amanda Newark has been studying penguins as part of a project run by the

[**9**]

Scientists have found some evidence of what is known as

[**10**] amongst penguins in Antarctica.

Amanda explains that the relationship between heart rate

and [**11**] is similar in penguins and humans.

In the experiment she describes, Amanda placed a

[**12**] containing a sensor in a penguin's nest.

Amanda explains that, for this experiment, it wasn't necessary to

[**13**] the penguins.

To identify the penguin she had approached, Amanda put

[**14**] on its front.

Amanda found that the penguin's heart rate increased when groups of

more than [**15**] humans approached it.

Larger groups of people did not upset the penguin as long as

they remained [**16**] when they were close to it.

Amanda feels that the arrangements made by

[**17**] have been very good so far.

Part 3

You will hear the owner of a very unusual house, and his architect, talking to a visitor to the house. For questions **18–22**, choose the answer (**A**, **B**, **C** or **D**) which fits best according to what you hear.

---

18 The owner feels that contemporary architecture

A has been impressive in London.
B is better than it used to be.
C has provided beautiful things to look at.
D produces work of lasting value.

	18

19 For the owner, one problem of living in the house is

A the position of the kitchen.
B the state of the walls.
C the number of storeys.
D the size of the rooms.

	19

20 The architect thinks the original builders were economical because they

A used readily available materials.
B dug extensive foundations.
C chose a soft piece of ground.
D built on a flat piece of land.

	20

21 The present kitchen was originally used for

A keeping provisions.
B storing arms and weapons.
C dining and entertaining.
D holding prisoners.

	21

22 The architect feels he has

A improved on the original design.
B preserved the original function.
C left a puzzle for future generations.
D given the house a viable future.

	22

Part 4

You will hear part of a radio discussion between two people, Louisa and William, who have been to a new modern art museum. For questions **23–28**, decide whether the opinions are expressed by only one of the speakers, or whether the speakers agree.

Write **L** for Louisa,
W for William,
or **B** for Both, where they agree.

---

23 It is not easy to find your way round the museum. [ ] 23

24 The title of the main exhibition reflects current ideas in art. [ ] 24

25 True art need not provoke an extreme reaction. [ ] 25

26 The sculpture at the entrance is of doubtful artistic value. [ ] 26

27 The exhibition is too showy. [ ] 27

28 Art should sometimes be soothing. [ ] 28

PAPER 5 SPEAKING (19 minutes)

There are two examiners. One (the interlocutor) conducts the test, providing you with the necessary materials and explaining what you have to do. The other examiner (the assessor) will be introduced to you, but then takes no further part in the interaction.

Part 1 (3 minutes)

The interlocutor first asks you and your partner a few questions which focus on information about yourselves and personal opinions.

Part 2 (4 minutes)

In this part of the test you and your partner are asked to talk together. The interlocutor places a set of pictures on the table in front of you. There may be only one picture in the set or as many as seven pictures. This stimulus provides the basis for a discussion. The interlocutor first asks an introductory question which focuses on two of the pictures (or in the case of a single picture, on aspects of the picture). After about a minute, the interlocutor gives you both a decision-making task based on the same set of pictures.

The picture for Part 2 is on page C3 of the colour section.

Part 3 (12 minutes)

You are each given the opportunity to talk for two minutes, to comment after your partner has spoken and to take part in a more general discussion.

The interlocutor gives you a card with a question written on it and asks you to talk about it for two minutes. After you have spoken, your partner is first asked to comment and then the interlocutor asks you both another question related to the topic on the card. This procedure is repeated, so that your partner receives a card and speaks for two minutes, you are given an opportunity to comment and a follow-up question is asked.

Finally, the interlocutor asks some further questions, which leads to a discussion on a general theme related to the subjects already covered in Part 3.

The cards for Part 3 are on pages C2 and C10 of the colour section.

Test 2

PAPER 1 READING (1 hour 30 minutes)

Part 1

For questions **1–18**, read the three texts below and decide which answer (**A**, **B**, **C** or **D**) best fits each gap.

Mark your answers **on the separate answer sheet.**

Citizen Kane

When the film *Citizen Kane* finally appeared in 1941, despite the brouhaha that attended its **(1)** .... – delayed because of distributors' fears of the harm William Randolph Hearst, its **(2)** .... subject, might do to them – and largely ecstatic reviews, it was not a commercial success. It was television that brought it back to the public consciousness. It is perhaps the one film, above all others, that has inspired people to become film-makers. This is all the more astonishing since it was Orson Welles's first film. Welles always **(3)** .... that its success arose from his having no idea of what he was or wasn't allowed to do: he just went ahead and did it. But he had an extraordinary team at his **(4)** ...., cameraman Gregg Toland, screenwriter Herman J. Mankiewicz, and the special-effects wizard Linwood Dunn. When Welles and Mankiewicz **(5)** .... on the idea of portraying a newspaper magnate who both was and wasn't Hearst, Welles realised that he had found a perfect vehicle for himself both as director and actor, and **(6)** .... his chance with the energy of a whirlwind.

1	**A** issue	**B** release	**C** publication	**D** broadcast
2	**A** attested	**B** admitted	**C** alleged	**D** affirmed
3	**A** maintained	**B** upheld	**C** detailed	**D** specified
4	**A** disposal	**B** invitation	**C** hand	**D** option
5	**A** latched	**B** jumped	**C** caught	**D** hit
6	**A** gripped	**B** plucked	**C** seized	**D** wrenched

Dermot and Carmel

Dermot thought that Carmel was rather odd that morning. Twice he had said that he might be late and not to worry if he **(7)** .... into the golf club on the way home. He had to have a natter with someone and that was the best place to have it. Twice she had **(8)** .... her head amiably and distantly as if she hadn't really heard or understood.

'Will you be all right? What are you going to do today?' he had asked.

She had smiled. 'Funny you should ask that. I was just thinking that I hadn't anything to do all day so I was going to **(9)** .... down town and look at the shops. I was thinking that it was almost a sinful thing, just **(10)** .... away the day.'

Dermot had smiled back. 'You're **(11)** .... to enjoy yourself. And as I said, if I'm late I won't want anything to eat. So don't **(12)** .... to any trouble.'

'No, that's fine,' she said.

7	**A** fell	**B** bumped	**C** dropped	**D** cut
8	**A** nodded	**B** gestured	**C** shrugged	**D** stirred
9	**A** pace	**B** tread	**C** step	**D** stroll
10	**A** drifting	**B** killing	**C** easing	**D** idling
11	**A** sanctioned	**B** entitled	**C** justified	**D** rightful
12	**A** take	**B** get	**C** go	**D** put

Title Race

Tea boy? Do you mind, I'm a mobile lukewarm beverage resource facilitator.

Human nature provides the most divine of comedies. **(13)** .... a recent study which has informed the nation that job titles are a prime cause of envy and unrest at work. A survey by a leading firm of recruitment consultants found that 90% of employers and 70% of employees admit that titles create **(14)** .... among colleagues.

Most shockingly, the survey found that 70% of office workers would be willing to **(15)** .... a pay rise in favour of a more 'motivational' or 'professional' job title. If our vanity is **(16)** .... such proportions that even basic greed is being overwhelmed, we are indeed in dire straits.

The truth is that in these brave new days of the early twenty-first century, nobody is content to be **(17)** .... subordinate. The titles under discussion **(18)** .... the emphasis on ability (specialist, coordinator) but are, in fact, little more than euphemisms.

13	**A** Corroborate	**B** Testify	**C** Confirm	**D** Witness
14	**A** compartments	**B** demarcations	**C** divisions	**D** partitions
15	**A** forgo	**B** revoke	**C** forbear	**D** resign
16	**A** attaining	**B** reaching	**C** touching	**D** finding
17	**A** defined	**B** marked	**C** labelled	**D** identified
18	**A** place	**B** set	**C** fix	**D** allocate

Part 2

You are going to read four extracts which are all concerned in some way with modern technology. For questions **19–26**, choose the answer (**A**, **B**, **C** or **D**) which you think fits best according to the text.

Mark your answers **on the separate answer sheet.**

Writing by hand and on screen

Dr Johnson maintained that 'what is written without effort is in general read without pleasure'. The converse is that good writing comes hard. Looking back through my handwritten school essays I was surprised at how few crossings-out they contained. Today I would have rewritten them five times over. I am sure the reason was that they were physically hard to write. The slowness of the hand disciplined the brain. What would be difficult to alter or erase was written with care. The casual facility of the computer leads to sloppiness. Most writers using word processors find the time spent correcting early drafts more or less equates with the time originally spent on handwritten text.

Equally, the e-mail, unlike the handwritten letter, is emotionally ponderous. This electronic Eros is said to have revived the art of the love letter. Millions of these missives now flow down the lines, where previously there was only idle chatter. Hurrah for that. At least these e-mails are written, in a sort of English and a sort of grammar. But words printed on a screen pack a monotonous punch. Their writers are often unaccustomed to the power of the written word and tend, in computer jargon, to 'flare'. Their meaning becomes exaggerated and distorted in transmission. And printed words written in haste lack the care and character of handwriting.

19 What point does the writer feel is illustrated by his school essays?

- **A** It is a mistake to change what you have written too many times.
- **B** The standard of what you write is better if it cannot easily be changed.
- **C** Word processors give writers a false impression of the quality of what they have written.
- **D** Computers make writers change their view concerning what constitutes good writing.

20 Which of the following does the writer imply about e-mails?

- **A** It is unlikely that they will remain a common way of sending love letters.
- **B** They are sometimes entertaining rather than informative.
- **C** They bear some relation to handwritten letters.
- **D** It is common for people to include computer terminology in them.

The CD

I put down my cup and went to inspect the CD. The case was disappointing but the rainbow-silver disc inside looked interesting.

'Wonderful little things, aren't they?' Mr Warriston said, coming back into the room. I agreed, gingerly handing the disc to him. 'Amazing they manage to squeeze seventy minutes of music onto them,' he continued, bending to the hi-fi device. He switched it on and all sorts of lights came on. He pressed a button and a little drawer slid out of the machine. He put the disc inside, pressed the button again and the tray glided back in again. 'Of course, some people say they sound sterile, but I think they...'

'Do you have to turn them over, like records?' I asked.

'What? No,' Mr Warriston said, straightening. 'No, you only play one side.'

'Why?' I asked him.

He looked nonplussed, and then thoughtful. 'You know,' he said, 'I've no idea. I don't see why you couldn't make both sides playable and double the capacity...' He stared down at the machine. 'You could have two lasers, or just turn it over by hand... hmm.' He smiled at me. 'Yes, good point.' He nodded over at my wooden chair. 'Anyway. Come on, let's get you sitting in the best place for the stereo effect, eh?'

I smiled, pleased to have thought of a technical question Mr Warriston could not answer.

21 What do we learn about the narrator from the extract?

A He was keen to prove that Mr Warriston could be wrong about some things.
B He was not very good at understanding technical matters.
C He already had a low opinion of CDs.
D He had never operated a CD player himself.

22 What do we learn about Mr Warriston from the extract?

A He liked to be knowledgeable about how machines worked.
B He found the narrator's questions annoying.
C He was more impressed by the way CDs worked than the sound they made.
D He was pretending to know a great deal about CDs.

Books versus Electronic Text

In comparing books and electronic text, the author Malcolm Bradbury was spot on when he said that if matches had been invented after cigarette lighters, we'd have marvelled at the improvement. Most of the propaganda, dazzled by newness, states that electronic text is a change comparable to the invention of printing and that it is already nearly completed. It ignores the fact that shifts in consciousness take generations and such rhetoric falls into the trap of chronocentricity, the egotism that one's own generation sits on the very cusp of history. Take this treasure from *Mighty Micro*, a book from 1979: 'The 1980s will see the book as we know it, and as our ancestors created and cherished it, begin a slow and steady slide to oblivion.' So far, so wrong. Reading anything lengthy on a screen is such a miserable experience that most never do it and, in any case, the organisation of what resides in computers encourages people to dip into text. Techno-proselytisers have extracted virtue here by claiming that inherent flightiness leads to new forms of narrative and imaginative space. But there's nothing new about 'non-linearity'. Lots of books have never been read from beginning to end – most religious texts, dictionaries and poetry collections spring to mind. What is new is not so much the branchings of electronic text as that computers don't invite the joined-up thinking of reading anything in its entirety.

23 The writer uses the quote from *Mighty Micro* to illustrate

- **A** the speed at which propaganda can have an effect.
- **B** people's tendency to overlook the disadvantages of change.
- **C** people's desire to feel that they are living in a period of great change.
- **D** the view on new inventions expressed by Malcolm Bradbury.

24 The writer implies that electronic text will not completely replace books because

- **A** it is not suited to people's desire to read some things all the way through.
- **B** it will lead to a style of writing that many people will find unappealing.
- **C** only certain kinds of books will be presented in the form of electronic text.
- **D** dipping into text can require more effort than reading something right through.

The Office

Charles walked through the office door and into a perfect world of order. The carpet was clear of the paper avalanche which had buried it on the very day it was put down, and the naked desk was dark wood, just as he remembered it from the Sotheby's auction of five weeks ago. Neat file-holders were being put in their proper drawers. Twelve years of trade journals now filled the shelves on one wall.

Kathleen strained to close the door of the filing cabinet and then turned on him. 'You have to go to computers, Charles. This is just too much.'

'Hello, Kathleen. Oh, this is amazing.' He was admiring the room, its antique furniture. He was not visualising a computer or any other mechanical device in it, not even a pencil sharpener. 'Simply amazing,' he said, altogether skirting the issue of computers.

Over the two years he had known her, they'd had this conversation many times. She could never understand his resistance to the technology when he was so adept at computers and had even published an important paper on computer-mode giftedness. She had been the inspiration for that paper. Via the keyboard, she could dip her fingers into the stuffing of any software and make it into a new animal that could sit up and bark at the moon if she wished.

25 What particularly pleased Charles when he first entered the office?

- **A** Kathleen was working hard to tidy it up.
- **B** The furniture had been rearranged.
- **C** There were no longer any mechanical devices there.
- **D** Its decor was now clearly visible.

26 What do we learn about Kathleen from this extract?

- **A** She did things on computer that Charles did not approve of.
- **B** She could do things with computers that Charles considered exceptional.
- **C** She had computer skills that even Charles could not understand.
- **D** She had become resigned to Charles's attitude to computers.

Part 3

You are going to read an extract from a book. Seven paragraphs have been removed from the extract. Choose from the paragraphs **A–H** the one which fits each gap (**27–33**). There is one extra paragraph which you do not need to use.

Mark your answers **on the separate answer sheet.**

The Vienna Assignment

I was in Vienna to take photographs. That was generally the reason I was anywhere then. Photographs were more than my livelihood. They were part of my life. The way light fell on a surface never failed to tug at my imagination. The way one picture, a single snapshot, could capture the essence of a time and place, a city, a human being, was embedded in my consciousness.

27

I'd come close once, when some weird aptness in the knotted shape of a smoke plume from a burning oil well made my picture the one newspapers and magazines all over the world suddenly wanted. Brief glory from an even briefer moment. Just luck, really. But they say you make your own – the bad as well as the good.

28

But, still, I was taking photographs. And I was being paid to do it. It didn't sound bad to me. The assignment was actually a piece of happenstance. I'd done the London shots for a glossy coffee-table picture book: *Four Cities in Four Seasons – London, Paris, Rome, Vienna*, a European co-publishing venture that netted me a juicy commission to hang round moody locations in my home city in spring, summer, autumn, and winter. I'd given my own particular slant to daffodils in Hyde Park and heat haze and traffic fumes in Piccadilly.

29

It was just after an obliging cold snap over Christmas and New Year that I handed in my London-in-winter batch and got the message that the Austrian photographer, Rudi Schüssner, had walked out on the job in Vienna for reasons nobody seemed to think I needed to know about. Rather than call in someone new, they offered me the substitute's role.

30

They put me up at the Europa, on Neuer Markt, in the heart of the old city. I'd last been to Vienna for a long weekend with my wife: a midsummer tourist scramble round just about every palace and museum in the joint. It had been hot, hectic and none too memorable. I hadn't even taken many photographs. On my own, in a cold hard January, it was going to be different, though.

31

The first day I didn't even try. I rode the trams round the Ringstrasse, getting on and off as I pleased to sample the moods of the place. The weather was set, frozen like the vast baroque remnants of the redundant empire that had laid the city out. I hadn't seen what Schüssner had done with spring, summer or autumn. I hadn't wanted to.

32

Next morning, I was out at dawn. Snow flurries overnight meant Stephansplatz would be virginally white as well as virtually deserted. I hadn't figured out how to cope with the cathedral in one shot. Its spire stretched like a giraffe's neck into the silver-grey sky, but at ground level it was elephantine, squatting massively in the centre of the city. Probably there was no way to do it. I'd have to settle for something partial. In that weather, at that time, it could still be magical. But then, there's always been something magical about photography.

33	

And even when you know why it happens you don't lose the sense of its mystery. That stays with you for ever. Perhaps that's why what happened at Stephansplatz that morning failed in some strange way to surprise me.

A The Austrian publishers had liked what they'd seen of my stuff, apparently. Besides, I was free, whereas the French and Italian photographers weren't. And I was glad to go. Things at home weren't great. They were a long way short of that. A week snapping snowy Vienna didn't have to be dressed up as a compliment to my artistry for me to go like a shot.

B This was going to be my Vienna, not his. And it was going to give itself to me. I just had to let it come. A photograph is a moment. But you have to wait for the moment to arrive. So I bided my time and looked and looked until I could see clearly. And then I was ready.

C I'd always shied clear of accessories, arguing that all you needed to do the job were a good pair of eyes and a decent camera. Plus spontaneity of course, which you don't get fiddling with tripod legs. I just prowled round the square, looking for the right angle, for some way to give scale as well as atmosphere to the scene.

D It certainly seemed that way to the nineteenth-century pioneers, before the chemistry of it was properly understood. Pictures develop and strengthen and hold by an agency of their own. You can stand in a darkened room and watch a blank sheet of paper become a photograph.

E I went freelance after that, which should have been a clever move and would probably have worked out that way, but for life beyond the lens taking a few wrong turnings. The mid-nineties weren't quite the string of triumphs I'd foreseen when my defining image made it to the cover of *Time* magazine. That's why I was in Vienna, rather than anywhere even faintly newsworthy.

F I'd also reconciled myself to the best and truest of what I'd delivered being tossed aside. It was, after all, only a picture book. It wasn't meant to challenge anyone's preconceptions or make them see instead of look.

G One day, one second, I might close the shutter on the perfect photograph. There was always the chance, so long as there was film in my camera. Finish one; load another; and keep looking, with eyes wide open. That was my code. Had been for a long time.

H I knew that the moment I climbed off the shuttle bus from the airport and let my eyes and brain absorb the pinky-grey dome of light over the snow-sugared roofs of the city. I was going to enjoy myself here. I was going to take some great pictures.

Part 4

You are going to read an extract from a novel. For questions **34–40**, choose the answer (**A**, **B**, **C** or **D**) which you think fits best according to the text.

Mark your answers **on the separate answer sheet**.

Simon Costello knew that the purchase of the house in Pembroke Square had been a mistake within a year of his and Lois's moving in. A possession which can only be afforded by the exercise of stringent and calculated economy is best not afforded at all. But at the time it had seemed a sensible, as well as a desirable, move. He had had a run of successful cases and they were coming in with reassuring regularity. Lois had returned to her job at the advertising agency within two months of the birth of the twins, and had been given a rise which took her salary to thirty-five thousand. It was Lois who had argued the more strongly for a move, but he had put up little resistance to arguments which at the time had seemed compelling: the flat wasn't really suitable for a family; they needed more room, a garden, separate accommodation for an au pair. All these, of course, could have been achieved in a suburb or in a less fashionable part of London than Pembroke Square, but Lois was ambitious for more than additional space. Mornington Mansions had never been an acceptable address for an up-and-coming young barrister and a successful businesswoman. She never said it without a sense that even speaking the words subtly diminished her standing, socially and economically.

Lois had decided that a necessary economy was for one of them to travel by public transport. Her firm was on the other side of London; obviously Simon must be the one to economise. The overcrowded tube journey, started in a mood of envious resentment, had become an unproductive thirty minutes of brooding on present discontents. He would recall his grandfather's house in Hampstead where he had stayed as a boy, the smell of dinner from the kitchen, his grandmother's insistence that the returning breadwinner, tired from his exhausting day in court, should be given peace, a little gentle cosseting, and relief from every petty domestic anxiety. She had been a 'lawyer's wife', indefatigable in legal good causes, elegantly present at all lawyers' functions, apparently content with the sphere of life which she had made her own. Well, that world had passed for ever. Lois had made it plain before their marriage that her career was as important as his. It hardly needed saying; this was, after all, a modern marriage. The job was important to her and important to them both. The house, the au pair, their whole standard of living depended on two salaries. And now what they were precariously achieving could be destroyed by that self-righteous, interfering Venetia.

Venetia must have come straight from the court to their offices and she had been in a dangerous mood. Something or someone had upset her. But the word 'upset' was too weak, too bland for the intensity of furious disgust with which she had confronted him. Someone had driven her to the limit of her endurance. He cursed himself. If he hadn't been in his room, if he'd only left a minute earlier, the encounter wouldn't have taken place, she would have had the night to think it over, to consider what, if anything, she ought to do. Probably nothing. The morning might have brought sense. He remembered every word of her angry accusations. **line 5**

'I defended Brian Cartwright today. Successfully. He told me that when you were his counsel four years ago you knew before trial that he had bribed three of the jury. You did nothing. You went on with the case. Is that true?'

'He's lying. It isn't true.'

'He also said that he passed over some shares in his company to your fiancée. Also before trial. Is that true?'

'I tell you, he's lying. None of it's true.'

The denial had been as instinctive as an arm raised to ward off a blow and had sounded unconvincing even to his own ears. His whole action had been one of guilt. The first cold horror draining his face was succeeded by a hot flush, bringing back shameful memories of his headmaster's study, of the terror of the inevitable punishment. He had made himself look into her eyes and had seen the look of contemptuous disbelief. If only he'd had some warning. He knew now what he should have said: 'Cartwright told me after the trial but I didn't believe him. I don't believe him now. That man will say anything to make himself important.'

But he had told a more direct, more dangerous lie, and she had known that it was a lie. Even so, why the anger, why the disgust? What was that old misdemeanour to do with her? Who had sent Venetia Aldridge to be guardian of the conscience of their legal practice? Or of his, come to that? Was her own conscience so clear, her behaviour in court always immaculate? Was she justified in destroying his career? And it would be destruction. He wasn't sure what exactly she could do, how far she was prepared to go, but if this got about, even as a rumour, he was done for.

34 One reason why Simon Costello had agreed to buy the house in Pembroke Square was that

A Lois persuaded him that he had a tendency to be too cautious.
B the idea arose at a time when he was optimistic about his earning capacity.
C he had not dared to dispute the reasons Lois had given him for doing so.
D he had felt that neither he nor Lois would have difficulty economising later.

35 One reason why Lois had wanted to buy the house was that

A she felt that Mornington Mansions reflected poorly on her status.
B Mornington Mansions was a place that other people had not heard of.
C she had never been happy living in Mornington Mansions.
D Mornington Mansions was in a particularly unpopular part of London.

36 Simon recalled that the atmosphere in his grandparents' house had been marked by

A his grandfather's dislike of everyday household matters.
B a clear understanding that his grandmother was the dominant figure there.
C apprehension as to what mood his grandfather would be in.
D his grandmother's understanding attitude towards his grandfather.

37 When Simon compared his own marriage with that of his grandparents, he

A was resentful that Lois did not have the same attitude as his grandmother.
B realised that his grandmother had been less content than she had seemed.
C wondered why he and Lois had not discussed her career plans more thoroughly.
D resigned himself to the fact that his own situation was inevitable.

38 Simon 'cursed himself' (line 51) when he thought about his confrontation with Venetia because

A he had failed to anticipate how angry she would be on her return from court.
B he had not given her time to reflect on the situation in a more measured way.
C he felt that it had been the result of nothing other than his own bad luck.
D he realised that he had not appreciated how much pressure she was under.

39 During the conversation about Brian Cartwright, Simon had

A looked like someone who was being dishonest.
B thought of responses but felt unable to give them.
C been puzzled as to why his responses had seemed dishonest.
D felt the need to control his own temper.

40 Which of the following did Simon wonder about Venetia?

A why she had such a good reputation
B whether she had something to hide
C why she liked spreading rumours
D whether she was acting out of character

PAPER 2 WRITING (2 hours)

Part 1

You **must** answer this question. Write your answer in **300–350** words in an appropriate style.

---

1 An area in the centre of your town is to be redeveloped. The Town Council has published the following suggestions and asked for proposals from residents. You decide to write a proposal addressed to the Town Council in which you discuss the advantages of **each** suggestion and justify your choice of **one** of the options.

Town Redevelopment

- a leisure centre, which will not only update the existing sports facilities, but also include new cinemas and restaurants
- a hotel and conference centre designed to attract visitors and increase opportunities for employment locally
- a supermarket with a multi-storey car park and some new homes for local people

Write your **proposal**.

Part 2

Write an answer to **one** of the questions **2–5** in this part. Write your answer in **300–350** words in an appropriate style.

---

2 A magazine is running a series entitled *Musical Memories*. Readers are invited to send in articles explaining why a piece of music reminds them of a particular occasion, and saying why the occasion is important to them.

Write your **article**.

3 A new magazine has been published to promote tourism in your country. Readers have been invited to send in reviews of an annual public event in their area, such as a festival. You decide to send in a review briefly describing your chosen event, and explaining its significance for local life and culture.

Write your **review**.

4 The following headline appeared in *Feelgood*, a lifestyle magazine, introducing an article about the attitudes of young people.

Being young – it's not fun

You decide to write a letter to the magazine based on your own experience, and giving reasons for your views.

Write your **letter**.

5 Based on your reading of **one** of these books, write on **one** of the following:

(a) Anne Tyler: *The Accidental Tourist*
Your local English-language newspaper has invited readers to send in reviews of books featuring characters who set about changing their lives. You decide to write a review of *The Accidental Tourist*, focusing on how Macon's character develops as a result of his misfortunes, finally allowing him to break free from his past.

Write your **review**.

(b) Brian Moore: *The Colour of Blood*
'Joy filled him. At last, he knew peace.' Write an essay for your tutor briefly describing the events that take place in the church at Rywald. You should analyse the reasons for Cardinal Bem's feelings at the end of the book.

Write your **essay**.

(c) L.P. Hartley: *The Go-Between*
Your local English-language newspaper is planning a series of articles on the role of the weather in fiction. You have read *The Go-Between* and decide to submit an article which assesses the importance of the weather to the story. You should consider how it affects the course of events at Brandham Hall.

Write your **article**.

PAPER 3 USE OF ENGLISH (1 hour 30 minutes)

Part 1

For questions **1–15**, read the text below and think of the word which best fits each space. Use only **one** word in each space. There is an example at the beginning **(0)**.

Write your answers in CAPITAL LETTERS **on the separate answer sheet**.

Example: | 0 | E | V | E | R | Y |

Advertising

Each and **(0)**..EVERY.. day we see hundreds of advertising images. **(1)**............ other kind of image confronts us **(2)**............ anything like the same frequency. Never in history **(3)**............ there been such a concentration of visual messages. The brain cannot help **(4)**............ take these messages in, and for a moment they stimulate the imagination **(5)**............ virtue of their appeal to memory or expectation.

Advertising is usually justified as a competitive medium of benefit **(6)**............ the public and efficient manufacturers. **(7)**............ it may be true that, in advertising, one particular brand competes against another, it is also just **(8)**............ true that such publicity images confirm and enhance others. That there are choices to be made **(9)**............ without saying but, ultimately, advertising as a system makes a single proposal – namely **(10)**............ we transform ourselves, or our lives, by buying something more. We are led to believe that, by **(11)**............ doing, we will in **(12)**............ way or another become richer – but in fact we will become poorer, **(13)**............ spent our money.

Advertising shows us people who have apparently been transformed into a new state and are, as a result, enviable. The state of being envied is **(14)**............ constitutes glamour. And advertising is in the business **(15)**............ manufacturing glamour.

Part 2

For questions **16–25**, read the text below. Use the word given in capitals at the end of some of the lines to form a word that fits in the space in the same line. There is an example at the beginning **(0)**.

Write your answers in CAPITAL LETTERS **on the separate answer sheet.**

Example: | **0** | I | N | T | E | L | L | E | C | T | U | A | L |

Science – is it only for the specialist?

There was a time when, as an educated person, you would have been expected	
to discuss any **(0)** INTELLECTUAL or cultural topic. You would have read the	**INTELLECT**
latest novel, been familiar with the work of poets, and been wholly **(16)**............	**CONVERSE**
with the current state of art and music. You would have felt equally relaxed	
discussing philosophical ideas in some **(17)**............ , should the subject of the	**DEEP**
discussion have changed. This would have meant the **(18)**............ of issues	**INCLUDE**
related to the results of scientific research.	
However, as significant discoveries accumulated, it became **(19)**............	**INCREASE**
difficult for any one person to keep abreast of developments across the entire	
field. A point was reached where the pace of progress was so great that a single	
brain became completely **(20)**............ to absorb the wealth of information.	**POWER**
Scientists could no longer **(21)**............ switch back and forth between	**CONFIDENCE**
disciplines as before. They became specialists.	
A broadly-educated person today can still have a general **(22)**............ of most	**AWARE**
of the specialisms, but not in the **(23)**............ detail in which research workers	**INTRICACY**
are themselves immersed. Trapped inside their own special areas, the pitfall for	
most research scientists is an **(24)**............ to communicate with those working	**ABLE**
on areas bordering their own, let alone totally **(25)**............ areas.	**CONNECT**

Part 3

For questions **26–31**, think of **one** word only which can be used appropriately in all three sentences. Here is an example **(0)**.

Example:

0 Some of the tourists are hoping to get compensation for the poor state of the hotel, and I think they have a very .... case.

There's no point in trying to wade across the river, the current is far too ....

If you're asking me which of the candidates should get the job, I'm afraid I don't have any .... views either way.

0	S	T	R	O	N	G											

Write **only** the missing word in CAPITAL LETTERS **on the separate answer sheet**.

---

26 Pia's under a lot of stress because she's in the .... of applying for a new job.

The company was trying to develop a new manufacturing .... in an attempt to cut costs.

Many people buy cosmetics in an attempt to slow down the .... of ageing.

27 The managing director would like to .... the candidates as a group before beginning the individual interviews.

I'm not sure what to do – it's not the sort of problem we expect to .... now we have all this modern technology.

The union officials said the management had agreed to .... the majority of their demands.

28 The party leaders got together to plan their next .... in the election campaign.

Chrysoula hated playing chess with Yannis because he always took so long when it was his ....

It's high time we made a .... : there's so much to do.

29 The censors cut one particular .... from the film before it was released.

I'd rather go to the cinema; I'm afraid opera isn't my ....

We couldn't get to sleep because we could hear the neighbours making a ....

30 After lunch, we had a .... of cards, just to pass the time.

His grandparents had a .... in Luca's upbringing, as his parents worked full-time.

Mrs Spencer opened the door and said, 'If you lay a .... on my son, there'll be trouble.'

31 The city is keen to shake off its .... as a post-industrial problem area.

It was only with the spread of cinemas in the 1920s that people began to regard the moving .... as a real art form.

Throughout the trial, Hopkins was the very .... of respectability.

Part 4

For questions **32–39**, complete the second sentence so that it has a similar meaning to the first sentence, using the word given. **Do not change the word given**. You must use between **three** and **eight** words, including the word given.

Here is an example **(0)**.

Example:

0 Do you mind if I watch you while you paint?

objection

Do you .... you while you paint?

0	*have any objection to my watching*

Write **only** the missing words **on the separate answer sheet**.

---

32 The police had to let the suspect go because new evidence was produced.

light

The police had to let the suspect go .... evidence produced.

33 The cost of building materials has gone up a great deal recently.

sharp

There has been .... building materials recently.

34 Maria didn't tell John the news until he had finished his meal.

for

Maria .... telling him the news.

35 Don't let her relaxed manner deceive you; she's an extremely shrewd businesswoman!

taken

Don't let .... her relaxed manner; she's an extremely shrewd businesswoman!

36 Unless the weather changes dramatically overnight, we'll be leaving at dawn.

no

Providing .... the weather overnight, we'll be leaving at dawn.

37 Werner found it hard to get used to the fact that he'd lost his job.

terms

Werner found it hard .... the fact that he'd lost his job.

38 Simon does not intend to visit his aunt again.

has

Simon .... his aunt again.

39 They gave Despina the impression that she would win first prize.

believe

Despina .... she would win first prize.

Part 5

For questions **40–44**, read the following texts on journalism. For questions **40–43**, answer with a word or short phrase. You do not need to write complete sentences. For question **44**, write a summary according to the instructions given.

Write your answers to questions **40–44 on the separate answer sheet**.

The news business relies heavily on high technology, but there is nothing scientific about it. 'Feel' is the oldest tool in journalism. Journalists are guided by hunch, gut instinct and assumptions dating back to the dawn of civilisation. This is admirably demonstrated in Evelyn Waugh's novel *Scoop*, written in 1936, in which two journalists are sent off to report on a war in a far distant country, foreign correspondents called away from journalistic jobs, which each knows are more important. At home, one covered politics and scandal, and the other wrote about the countryside. This order of priorities hasn't changed much, I fear. **line 8**

News is about the exceptional, something which threatens, benefits, outrages, enlightens, titillates or amuses. Preferably it carries a headline: 'Pop star becomes astronaut!' or 'Killer bees invade small town!'. But it might also be a slow pattern of details, like a deadly virus gradually spreading into a worldwide epidemic.

There is no shortage of news reports. An average newspaper editor might sift through a million words of news daily, but have room for only a few thousand. Decisions are not made about what is fit to print. They are about what fits. And where space is tight, news from far away is always the loser.

40 According to the writer, what is paradoxical in the first paragraph about the process of news production?

....

41 Which phrase later in the text echoes the idea behind 'This order of priorities hasn't changed much'? (line 8)

....

Newspaper reporters must often work on their own, but some prefer the security of comparing notes with those from other organisations. The result can be the lies and trash of which the tabloids are often accused, but in the quality press this is, in my opinion, rare and exceptional.

Why? Because the reporting of news is not a series of 'almost random reactions to random events', to use a much misused quote. It is a highly organised, systematic response based on years of personal experience among senior journalists. This is, of course, an artificial human invention, because there are no God-given, ultimate, objective means of measuring news priorities. But it is one to which most journalists and most broadcasters bring a strong sense of public responsibility.

Journalists may often be unaware of the way their own social status or personal beliefs can affect their judgements or their phrasing. Consciously or unconsciously, however, they generally base their choice and treatment of news on two criteria: firstly, what is the political, social, economic and human significance of the event, and secondly, will it interest, excite and entertain the readers? The first takes precedence over the second, but both matter. No newspaper can succeed unless it strikes a chord with its readers and keeps in tune with them.

42 Which **two** phrases in the text reflect a very negative view of newspaper articles and their contents?

....

43 In your own words, explain how an individual reporter's social status or personal beliefs can affect his or her reporting.

....

44 In a paragraph of **50–70** words, summarise **in your own words as far as possible** the basis on which news stories are selected for publication, as described in **both** texts. Write your summary **on the separate answer sheet**.

PAPER 4 LISTENING (40 minutes approximately)

Part 1

You will hear four different extracts. For questions **1–8**, choose the answer (**A**, **B** or **C**) which fits best according to what you hear. There are two questions for each extract.

Extract One

You hear a woman talking about tourism.

1 What characterised the holidays provided by tour companies in the late twentieth century?

A They were tailored to the particular destination.
B They had inadequate safety precautions.
C They were in a predictably uniform environment.

	1

2 Why did the tourists fail to find out about the countries they visited?

A The resorts were in isolated places.
B Tour companies made no provision for this.
C Host countries were unprepared for them.

	2

Extract Two

You hear a woman talking about a 16th-century map of London.

3 The map is not a true reflection of London because

A the only public buildings shown were churches.
B the pieces of the map did not make up a whole.
C the map-makers had limited drawing skills.

	3

4 What was the main purpose of the map?

A to patronise the arts
B to promote business in the city
C to reflect the buyers' status

	4

Extract Three

You hear part of a radio discussion about a new film.

5 What do the speakers agree about?

A the reason for making the film
B the effectiveness of the action scenes
C the inadequacy of the script

	5

6 What is the man's main criticism of the film?

A It lacks suspense.
B It lacks direction.
C It lacks originality.

	6

Extract Four

You hear part of a radio programme about the 18th-century composer Handel.

7 According to the speaker, Handel's operas were, until recently, regarded as

A models for modern composers.
B too conventional to stage.
C historical curiosities.

	7

8 The speaker feels that the rigid 18th-century musical conventions can be

A used to emphasise the emotions of the singers.
B overcome by the development of modern singing styles.
C made less effective by different staging and direction.

	8

Part 2

You will hear part of a radio programme about the difficulties faced by witnesses and by the police after a crime has been committed. For questions **9–17**, complete the sentences with a word or short phrase.

Witnesses often need to remember details of fast-moving events which happened in very [**9**] situations.

A [**10**] analysis was the basis of the old 'photofit' identity system.

Witnesses now build up facial features on a [**11**] to create a good likeness.

The police practice of conducting [**12**] has not proved very successful.

Witnesses are generally more able to recognise someone of the same [**13**] from among the suspects.

Surprisingly, the [**14**] of witnesses is not always a good indication of their reliability.

Experiments have shown that [**15**] memory deteriorates in older people.

Older people are often confused about the [**16**] of their memory.

Additional communication problems between police and witnesses may be caused by both age and [**17**] differences.

Part 3

You will hear a radio interview with Diana Boardman, the manager of an orchestra.
For questions **18–22**, choose the answer (**A**, **B**, **C** or **D**) which fits best according to what you hear.

---

18 Diana feels that her orchestra is special because

A it benefits from a long history.
B her players are skilled in many areas.
C it is known for a particular type of music.
D she has associated with the right people.

	18

19 Diana says that her concerts

A are better attended than most.
B consist of a mix of music types.
C can be interpreted in two ways.
D have a high risk element to them.

	19

20 According to Diana, it is important to

A move towards a change in musical traditions.
B distinguish classical music from other art forms.
C understand the past influences on music.
D recognise the role of women in the history of music.

	20

21 Diana feels that the number of men in classical music audiences

A should come as no surprise.
B is generally underestimated.
C reflects how things have changed.
D is difficult to explain.

	21

22 Why did Diana decide to make arts administration her career?

A It was a subject she had studied.
B It proved to be satisfying.
C She likes a competitive atmosphere.
D Influential colleagues recommended it.

	22

Part 4

You will hear Colin Beattie, the presenter of a radio arts programme, talking to Annie Watson, a critic, about a new TV drama series which stars an actor called Richard Garrard. For questions **23–28**, decide whether the opinions are expressed by only one of the speakers, or whether the speakers agree.

Write **A** for Annie,
C for Colin,
or **B** for Both, where they agree.

---

23 Garrard plays villains particularly well. [ ] **23**

24 There is little new about Garrard's latest role. [ ] **24**

25 One point in favour of the new series is its location. [ ] **25**

26 One part of the series has been successfully exploited for promotional purposes. [ ] **26**

27 The first episode of the series was quite moving at times. [ ] **27**

28 The new series moves at too leisurely a pace. [ ] **28**

PAPER 5 SPEAKING (19 minutes)

There are two examiners. One (the interlocutor) conducts the test, providing you with the necessary materials and explaining what you have to do. The other examiner (the assessor) will be introduced to you, but then takes no further part in the interaction.

Part 1 (3 minutes)

The interlocutor first asks you and your partner a few questions which focus on information about yourselves and personal opinions.

Part 2 (4 minutes)

In this part of the test you and your partner are asked to talk together. The interlocutor places a set of pictures on the table in front of you. There may be only one picture in the set or as many as seven pictures. This stimulus provides the basis for a discussion. The interlocutor first asks an introductory question which focuses on two of the pictures (or in the case of a single picture, on aspects of the picture). After about a minute, the interlocutor gives you both a decision-making task based on the same set of pictures.

The pictures for Part 2 are on pages C4–C5 of the colour section.

Part 3 (12 minutes)

You are each given the opportunity to talk for two minutes, to comment after your partner has spoken and to take part in a more general discussion.

The interlocutor gives you a card with a question written on it and asks you to talk about it for two minutes. After you have spoken, your partner is first asked to comment and then the interlocutor asks you both another question related to the topic on the card. This procedure is repeated, so that your partner receives a card and speaks for two minutes, you are given an opportunity to comment and a follow-up question is asked.

Finally, the interlocutor asks some further questions, which leads to a discussion on a general theme related to the subjects already covered in Part 3.

The cards for Part 3 are on pages C2 and C10 of the colour section.

Test 3

PAPER 1 READING (1 hour 30 minutes)

Part 1

For questions **1–18**, read the three texts below and decide which answer (**A**, **B**, **C** or **D**) best fits each gap.

Mark your answers **on the separate answer sheet.**

Amateur Astronomy

Many things have changed in astronomy over the past half-century. Until about 30 years ago, there was a great **(1)** .... of charts and catalogues. Telescopic equipment was limited and there were few books on practical astronomy. Today, the range of off-the-shelf telescopes and equipment covers almost everything one could need. Electronic calculators and computers have revolutionised almanacs and chart production, and **(2)** .... the analysis of observations and the publication of results.

All this must surely make this the golden **(3)** .... of amateur astronomy. Well, perhaps, but a great deal has been lost as well. Now one may have to travel 80 km to find a sky comparable to that found in urban areas 50 years ago. The daytime skies are now **(4)** .... by aircraft condensation trails which can **(5)** .... for hours and often spread out to form amorphous clouds, making solar observations impossible and **(6)** .... night-time observation too.

1	**A** deficiency	**B** shortfall	**C** inadequacy	**D** shortage
2	**A** facilitated	**B** maximised	**C** cultivated	**D** upheld
3	**A** period	**B** age	**C** time	**D** term
4	**A** bothered	**B** plagued	**C** troubled	**D** badgered
5	**A** proceed	**B** pursue	**C** prolong	**D** persist
6	**A** hampering	**B** smothering	**C** overcoming	**D** combating

Too Much Choice

Society is becoming 'overchoiced'. There are too many things to do, too many options, too many opportunities. In the new economy, the desire for the new product, service or next big thing is an addiction, and technology simply accelerates the **(7)** .... of change: the noise, the **(8)** .... of new goods and services, offering more and more choice. No sooner has the new product emerged off this virtual production line than the next one is about to be **(9)** ..... The head spins, the brain races, the fatigue **(10)** .... ; the disconnection from life begins.

Choice is the mantra of the new economy, but more choice means more stress, less time and more complexity. Hence a new trend is **(11)** ..... The search is on for 'simplexity' – the simple things that give meaning in an increasingly complex world. But simplifying your life is not easy in an age of economic excess. There are more basic brands of detergent and breakfast cereals than we can ever need or want, more software upgrades, features and calling plans than we can keep **(12)** .... of.

7	**A** motion	**B** step	**C** pace	**D** movement
8	**A** proliferation	**B** escalation	**C** extension	**D** augmentation
9	**A** initiated	**B** embarked	**C** instituted	**D** launched
10	**A** sets in	**B** gives in	**C** sets up	**D** gives up
11	**A** aground	**B** afoot	**C** abreast	**D** afire
12	**A** track	**B** sight	**C** trace	**D** hold

McAndrews Hotel

Every summer we spend a fortnight in McAndrews Hotel in North Mayo, Ireland. It is a family tradition, **(13)** .... by my grandmother, and by now it has achieved a certain sacredness. Nothing is allowed to interfere with the ritual. We are of a kind, McAndrews clientele: old-fashioned, odd perhaps, some would say snobbish. I do not like the bad manners, the insolence of shop assistants which **(14)** .... for egalitarianism in this present age; I resent chummy overtures from waiters who sometimes appear to **(15)** .... themselves with difficulty from slapping one on the back. I know most of my fellow-guests' names – like me they have been coming here since they were children – yet can **(16)** .... assured that when I meet any of them in any part of the hotel, I shall be spared all social intercourse **(17)** .... a civil word of greeting. Such respect for dignity and personal privacy is **(18)** .... to come by in commercial establishments these days.

13	**A** constructed	**B** prompted	**C** heralded	**D** instigated
14	**A** passes	**B** poses	**C** claims	**D** serves
15	**A** restrict	**B** repress	**C** restrain	**D** retract
16	**A** stand	**B** rest	**C** stay	**D** keep
17	**A** on top of	**B** rather than	**C** as much as	**D** apart from
18	**A** slow	**B** rare	**C** hard	**D** seldom

Part 2

You are going to read four extracts which are all concerned in some way with acting. For questions **19–26**, choose the answer (**A**, **B**, **C** or **D**) which you think fits best according to the text.

Mark your answers **on the separate answer sheet**.

The Actor's Craft

Derision and contempt are sprayed at actors from time to time. Much of this disdain is fuelled by the actors themselves when they're compelled by their film/theatre companies to talk about their craft (and themselves) in interviews. They should give the dancer Pavlova's reply to the man who asked her what she meant when she was dancing: 'If I could tell you,' she said, 'I wouldn't dance it.' But instead they all too easily fall into ponderous clichés, silly truisms or into the prurient jaws of the gossip machine. We should all pay heed to what Paul Scofield said in a letter to a friend of mine: 'I have found that an actor's work has life and interest only in its execution. It seems to wither away in discussion and become emptily theoretical and insubstantial. It has no rules (except perhaps audibility). With every play and every playwright the actor starts from scratch, as if he or she knows nothing and proceeds to learn afresh every time – growing with the relationships of the characters and the insights of the writer. When the play has finished its run, he's empty until the next time. And it's the emptiness which is, I find, apparent in any discussion of theatre work.'

19 What does Pavlova's remark reveal about artists and performance?

A Many artists are inarticulate.
B The performance speaks for itself.
C Artists are unwilling to share the secrets of their craft.
D Indirect comments best describe their work.

20 What justification does the writer find for the disrespect in which actors are held?

A Actors refuse to tell the truth about what they do.
B Actors tell interviewers what their employers want them to.
C Actors give interviewers the sense they are acting under compulsion.
D Actors are unable to avoid making inappropriate remarks.

A review of *Hamlet*

Adrian Lester's Hamlet is poised precariously between boyhood and manhood, and it is a performance of thrilling simplicity and assurance. His handling of the text and his physical and psychological self-control take him, in one leap, from brilliantly promising to frontline player: an actor with the intelligent confidence to be almost self-effacing. Lester plays an edgy, tetchy young man who feeds on a banked-down sense of anger; agile, watchful and driven, he deploys a sense of acid wit and generous humour that makes him both formidable and lovable. Although played down, the virtuosity of this performance is unmistakable. Observe Lester's body, the way his arms hang stiffly, giving you a sense of a figure waiting to be animated. Handy's portrayal of Horatio gives you a similar feeling of a body being moved by an inner force that he both knows and does not know. So what is acting? What is behaviour? Is the former an imitation or an evocation of the latter? Who and what animates these bodies, morally and physically? That is the central question about the life of the theatre.

21 How has Adrian Lester's status been affected by playing the role of Hamlet?

- **A** He is confident enough to act simply.
- **B** He continues to exhibit potential as a performer.
- **C** He can now be regarded as a mature actor.
- **D** He has no need to flaunt his skills.

22 In his performance of this role, Lester demonstrates

- **A** the power of anger on stage.
- **B** that great performances can be subdued.
- **C** the approach of a primarily comic actor.
- **D** that character emerges through interaction with others.

One director's approach to rehearsal

The first stage of this director's rehearsal process is known as 'dropping in', a procedure which goes something like this. The stage manager projects the script onto a screen. The actors sit quietly while someone else is speaking, finding out what effect the words are having. When it is their turn to speak, they glance at the screen, digest the first phrase, think about what it means to them, wait to find the impulse – the reason to speak – then speak. For example, the line is, 'Queuing all night, the rain, do you remember?' Breathe. Let the thought drop in with your breath. A memory, a vision, an impression. Some people will imagine a queue, maybe at a bus stop on the way to rehearsals or for a rock concert in their youth. Having visualised the scene, find the impulse to speak it – what this director calls 'the pathway to the line'. Impulses can come from without or within. Look in the eyes of the other actor listening. Consider your character's situation. This director talks of 'dropping in' as a means of finding out what is going on. Don't pre-plan or pre-judge. Dare to go down there with an empty mind and trust that something will happen to you.

23 What individual input is required of the actor in the method known as 'dropping in'?

- **A** to produce a mental image to support the words
- **B** to consider how the other actors are performing
- **C** to generate interaction with the other actors
- **D** to put trust in the director's method

24 Before the actors start 'dropping in', the director requires them to

- **A** study the whole text of the play.
- **B** work out a preliminary view of their part.
- **C** build up confidence about the eventual performance.
- **D** abandon all preconceptions about their role.

Visual materials for Paper 5

TEST 1

Prompt card 1a

Which is preferable – working for yourself or working for a big company?

- risks and rewards
- status
- personality

TEST 2

Prompt card 2a

How important is it to go away on holiday?

- relaxation
- learning
- variety

TEST 3

Prompt card 3a

How do the media help people to enjoy life?

- escapism
- knowledge
- variety

TEST 4

Prompt card 4a

What abilities does a leader need?

- knowledge
- social skills
- strength

TEST 1 PAPER 5 New website – Promoting cycling

TEST 2 PAPER 5 TV Series – Importance of the past

2A

2B

2C

2D

2E

Calendar promotion – Tourism

3A

3B

3C

3D

3E

3F

Book cover – Changing status of women

4A

4B

4C

4D

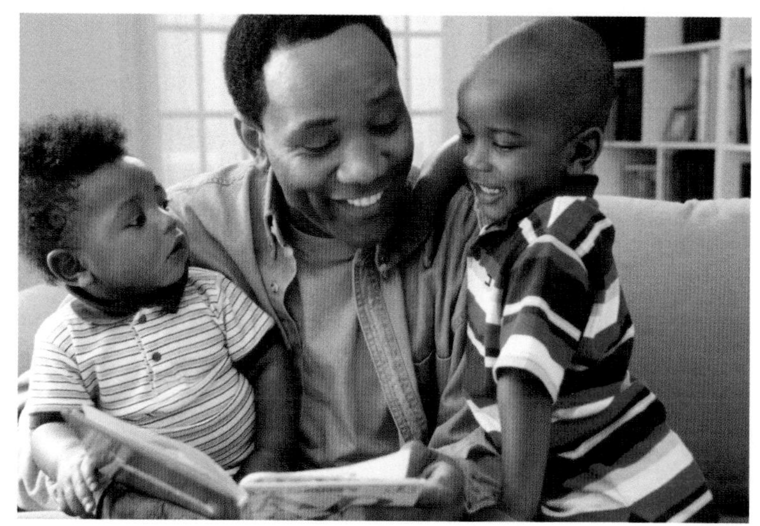

4E

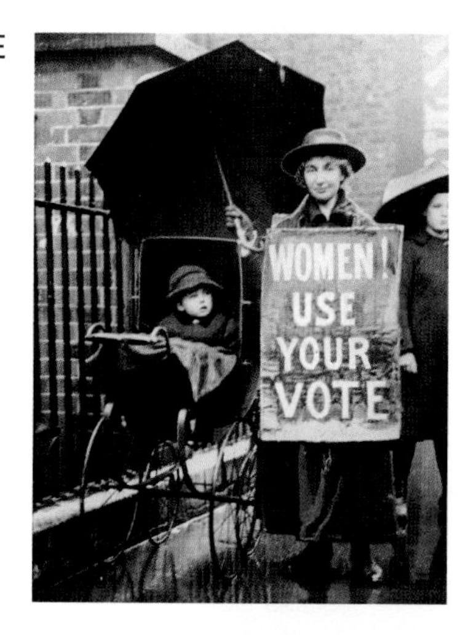
WOMEN!
USE
YOUR
VOTE

4F

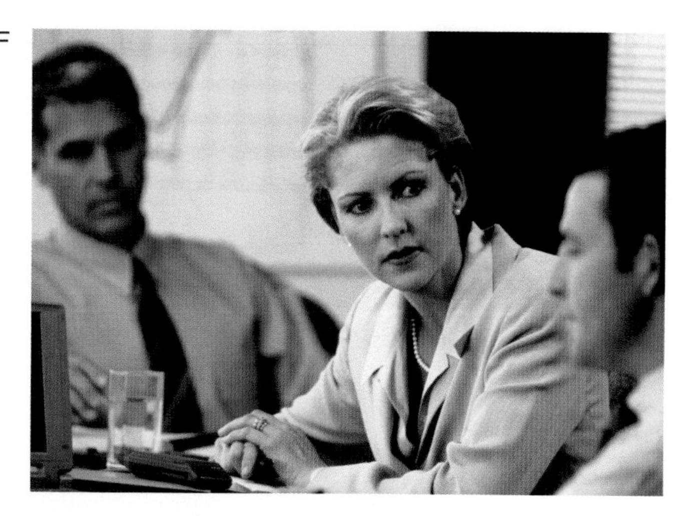

4G

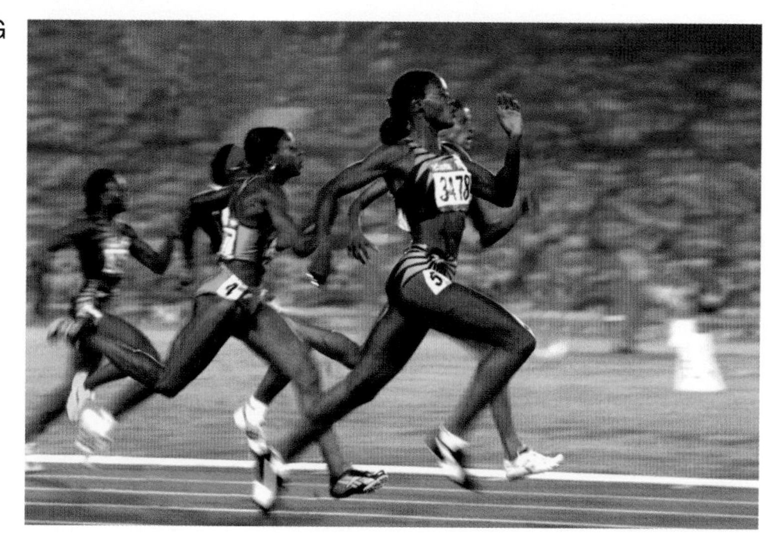
3478

TEST 1

Prompt card 1b

When interviewing applicants for a job, what do employers look for?

- **knowledge**
- **experience**
- **image**

TEST 2

Prompt card 2b

Which is a better way of escaping boredom, watching television or reading books?

- **time**
- **the subject**
- **imagination**

TEST 3

Prompt card 3b

What can affect people's enjoyment of city life?

- **atmosphere**
- **facilities**
- **size**

TEST 4

Prompt card 4b

What is the point of learning a foreign language?

- **work**
- **travel**
- **cultural reasons**

TEST 4

Prompt card 4c

Which is it more important to develop, creative or practical skills?

- **work**
- **home**
- **leisure**

The Perfect Theatre

The perfect theatre should make you feel as if your presence has made a difference. Going to the theatre, going to any live performance, is an event and the staff need to have a sense of that, too. It's terribly alienating if you feel that it's just any old job for the people working front of house.

The theatre itself needs to create a relationship between the performer and the audience – no one in the audience should feel that they're getting an unreasonably prejudiced view of the actor. It's important that they're not too far away, they can hear, they can see, they can feel in some sense in contact with what's going on on stage. The proportions of an auditorium are important. They have to respond to the human voice and the scale of the human body. If an auditorium dwarfs the human body, there's something wrong with it because you can't deny the human form at the heart of drama. A lot of theatres in the late nineteenth century got it right because they managed to shape an auditorium that somehow embraces the stage.

I like theatres that have a sense of the past in them. Like worn stone steps in a church, you get the sense of layers of human presence. From the point of view of the plays, you can't have something for everybody. You can't second-guess an audience because they don't know what they're going to want to see. When you visit the theatre, you want something done in a way you can't imagine, otherwise you may as well have stayed at home.

25 What does the writer regard as being essential from theatre personnel in contact with an audience?

- **A** an efficient approach to the job they do
- **B** treating members of the audience as individuals
- **C** a feeling that they too are also performers
- **D** fostering a feeling of a special occasion

26 Why might the audience lack involvement with a play?

- **A** They arrive with a negative viewpoint.
- **B** They do not have the seats they expected.
- **C** They are put off by the design of the theatre.
- **D** They fail to relate to the play being performed.

Part 3

You are going to read an extract from a newspaper article. Seven paragraphs have been removed from the extract. Choose from the paragraphs **A–H** the one which fits each gap (**27–33**). There is one extra paragraph which you do not need to use.

Mark your answers **on the separate answer sheet.**

Joanna's Lessons

Joanna MacGregor has a hectic schedule as a concert pianist. So why has she added the task of writing books for young children learning the piano?

Even a member of that mythical species, the completely tone deaf, could not fail to be stirred by a Joanna MacGregor performance. Simply to see her zipping around a keyboard grabbing fistfuls of notes at the behest of some unfeasible contemporary score is to watch a pianist pushing the human frame to its limits.

27 ______

How many veterans of the concert hall platform would be floored by such a request? For Joanna MacGregor, though, it was simply a hoot. 'In his eyes, until I played that, I hadn't passed the test. I wasn't a proper pianist.' Needless to say, she sailed through and doubtless logged the experience for her next children's recital.

28 ______

There hardly seems to be a festival this summer she is not gracing. Tomorrow she is in the thick of an all-day collaboration between nine young composers and artists. She runs her own recording label, Sound Circus. And by her own admission, she cannot meet an artist of any sort without being tempted to suggest a joint project. So why on earth take on the extra burden of writing a book?

29 ______

In producing the first three books, MacGregor is drawing on vivid experience. Between the ages of 18 and 25, before she was getting concert engagements as a pianist, she taught a stream of beginners the piano. But most important in her make-up now as a musician who is unsurpassed in the breadth of her eclectic repertoire was the endless procession of small boys and girls traipsing into her childhood home, where her mother taught the piano.

30 ______

Just as everyone should be able to learn how to swim or to speak a smattering of French, so, in her view, should everybody be able to make a stab at learning the piano. Some kids have a flair and make rapid progress. She is fascinated by the others: those who chug along at varying rates of progress, enjoying it for a while, but all too often giving up. This falling off happens at any stage. Some kids find the beginning too frustrating. Others rebel further down the line when the stakes get higher and parental pressure is driving them 'to be like those children on the telly'.

31 ______

The production of her own training manual begs an obvious question. Does she have a poor opinion of the existing corpus of tutor books, or indeed of the general quality of piano teaching? 'I'm very reluctant to criticise other people's teaching or others' tutor books,' she says. What she does do is readily accept that her books, colourful and eye-catching though they are, are by no means the only books on the market designed to make the first steps enjoyable.

32 ______

'You have to allow them to improvise and give them a reason to play at either end of the keyboard and on the black notes and use the pedals.' As progress is made, bigger obstacles loom. Children need to be coaxed quite hard to read the music rather than rely on ear. Having relied for so much of her own childhood on her very keen ear, MacGregor has considerable sympathy on this score.

33

'I have enormous sympathy with people who find it difficult. I don't think people talk about it enough.' The secret, whether you do it for twenty minutes or five hours, is to work out beforehand what it is you are aiming to do, she says. Other tips: treat yourself – play the whole piece through, however many wrong notes. And mix hard with easy.

A MacGregor is rare among top-flight concert pianists for the interest she takes in how young children learn the instrument. She has just published her own elementary piano tutor for children: *Joanna MacGregor's Piano World.* And she has managed it despite a crippling work schedule.

B But she believes the single most important factor is practice. How can children be persuaded to play a passage even once again, let alone many times over? She admits to not having practised rigorously until she went to the Royal Academy of Music, where she began building up a contemporary repertoire whose formidable difficulties demanded practice. Now she loves it. The eight hours a day that she gets through are the core of her musical life, she says, more important than performances.

C 'Not only was I fiddling around at the keyboard, but there were all these other children of all backgrounds wanting to play every sort of music – bits of classical, jazz, pop, improvisation. I wasn't part of that hothouse thing of forcing exceptional talent. I grew up with the idea of trying to make music available to people of all abilities.'

D Her own special wheeze for luring these neophytes, the fives, sixes and sevens, through those bewildering times is to weave a storyline into the books and their accompanying CDs. The challenge at this fragile stage is to make the work interesting. And so, from lesson one, there are accompaniments in a variety of styles for teacher – or parent – to play beneath a child's line. For kids whose parents aren't pianists the accompaniments are recorded on the CDs. Learning should be unadulterated fun, MacGregor insists.

E But even her dazzling virtuosity was not enough to wow one small boy at a recent concert she gave for kids. Like the rest of the audience, he had been cascaded with bits and bobs of pieces in every style from her vast repertoire of classical, jazz, ragtime, blues, techno, African, etc. He'd coolly watched her dive under the lid of the concert grand to pluck the wires – normally a surefire knockout for kids. Then as she drew breath and invited questions, he piped up: 'Can you play *Match of the Day*?'

F And so the odyssey begins. It's a long journey but the first task for the young enthusiasts is easy, find the Cs – they're always to the left of the two black keys. In Book 2, the characters fall inside the piano and open up opportunities for making a whole lot of weird noises. Something parents, unlike MacGregor and the youngsters, may find a strain on the eardrums.

G 'I worry that some people use music, like sport, as a way of making their children achieve things, rather than just saying: it's music, it's there to enjoy. The reason children fall by the wayside is because they feel they are not going to match up to their parents' expectations.'

H 'People who know me are clearly surprised. But I think the very first lessons are absolutely crucial. It says a lot about the music profession that we tend to concentrate on the top end, on this idea of the child as nascent virtuoso. Most people's interest in music is much more ordinary and everyday. I find that far more interesting.'

Part 4

You are going to read an extract from a novel. For questions **34–40**, choose the answer (**A**, **B**, **C** or **D**) which you think fits best according to the text.

Mark your answers **on the separate answer sheet**.

We are talking Big Boots here. Really BIGTIME Boots.

I stood in my 800-dollar-each designer-label cowboy boots on the rocks of an old formation in the Arizona desert sand. Money no object. I wore the whole truly cowboy outfit and if *you* had the outfit you might be a cowboy. But I was not. It wasn't working. I squinted into the morning sun looking out at the Arizona mountains and I had to admit, I was not at home on the range.

Flying in from Denver just after dawn, I had the feeling that I just might pass for an ol' cowhand coming in from the sky. The feeling didn't last past the first real cowboy in the luggage hall of Phoenix airport. He was wearing a sweat-stained T-shirt, needed a shave, and was hoisting a dirty canvas bag off the conveyer belt when he caught sight of my brand new cowboy boots. He slowly raised one eyebrow and moved off out of the door without looking back.

There ought to be, somewhere, hanging in a closet, a suit of clothes an ex-racing driver can put on without feeling like he is from another planet. Something he could wear so that wherever he goes he doesn't get the feeling that everybody is talking another language and doing whatever they do at half speed. I liked, no, not liked... I flatout *loved* being a racing driver, driving racing cars. I am addicted to it and it is all I know how to do. But I don't do it any more. I couldn't if I wanted to. Question is, I thought, looking into the mean, rust-coloured rock of the mountains in the distance, what do I do now?

A racing driver should have one or two fall-back identities lined up for when he climbs out of his car. I thought I did, but when I reached for them they just disappeared. How about: an ex-racing driver adds colour to the commentary direct from the trackside? 'We got fifteen guys, all of them former Indy and Formula One drivers, fifteen guys in front of you, Forrest, standing in line to be colour commentators. We'll call you.'

Well then, how about: an ex-racing driver joins a partnership to sell classic cars? That lasted nearly all winter with phone calls, lunches, lawyers and meetings with bankers. But it was the year nobody was buying old Ferraris and Honda was 'reviewing' its dealer list. So in the end I gracefully withdrew before there was nothing to withdraw from. Being an 'ex' anything is depressing work. I mean you tell me; how badly do you want to hear about how I was almost the World Champion? Nobody wants to hear a story that ends in 'almost'. And even if I had been world champion you could probably just about stand to listen to the story for five minutes before your ears turned to cement. Last year's champion was last year.

Not that I want sympathy. Which is just as well, since I don't get any. Well, why should I? I had a good run, made money and hung on to enough. But oh, man, I miss the heat of slipping into that graceful, elegant, shrink-wrapped super-tech machine with seven hundred horsepower behind my neck. Zero to a hundred and fifty miles an hour in 4.9 seconds. And yes, I miss coming within an eyelash of killing myself every race or so. I miss the bright and gorgeous people and the reporters who acted as if what I said mattered. Being famous, even in a minor way, isn't all bad. Businessmen and politicians bragged to their friends that they knew me. Little boys slid under fences to get my autograph. And now that I don't drive a racing car... Only last week the phone rang twice. I have time in the morning and I have time in the afternoon. And let me just check, but I think tomorrow is free. So much empty time.

I looked up into the soft blue morning sky. No buzzards overhead. Maybe Arizona doesn't have buzzards. But a couple of little brown birds in a saguaro cactus just in front of me were giving me advice; something like 'get away from our nest before we sing our hearts out'. It had never occurred to me that the desert had songbirds. It did occur to me that a bogus cowboy in designer boots had a lot to learn.

34 How did the cowboy at Phoenix airport react to the narrator's appearance?

- **A** He was shocked.
- **B** He was unimpressed.
- **C** He was angered.
- **D** He was disturbed.

35 According to the narrator, ex-racing drivers in the company of others feel a sense of

- **A** superiority.
- **B** pride.
- **C** alienation.
- **D** failure.

36 The narrator did not get the first new job he tried for because

- **A** he was not so well qualified as others.
- **B** his contacts had misinformed him.
- **C** he applied at short notice.
- **D** his experience was not unique.

37 Why did the narrator give up selling cars?

- **A** He could see the future of the operation was bleak.
- **B** He did not enjoy the constant entertaining involved.
- **C** He felt unequal to the demands of the job.
- **D** He did not feel comfortable as a salesman.

38 When the narrator was a racing driver, he

- **A** enjoyed having his opinions respected.
- **B** was embarrassed by the attention he received.
- **C** used his position to make influential contacts.
- **D** had occasional fears for his personal safety.

39 What impression does the narrator try to create by using the phrase 'And let me just check' in the penultimate paragraph?

- **A** that he regrets finishing as a racing driver
- **B** that he is not open to new opportunities
- **C** that he has a busy schedule
- **D** that he is not enjoying life

40 As he looked at the birds on the cactus, the narrator

- **A** came to terms with his new life.
- **B** realised the extent of his ignorance.
- **C** felt apprehensive about making a new start.
- **D** decided this was not the place for him.

PAPER 2 WRITING (2 hours)

Part 1

You **must** answer this question. Write your answer in **300–350** words in an appropriate style.

---

1 You see the announcement below on your college notice board and decide to submit a proposal.

> The college will be putting on an exhibition entitled *Great Achievers*. The exhibition will include famous people from all over the world who have made contributions to public life in, for example, the arts, the sciences, entertainment or sport.
>
> Please submit a proposal suggesting a person whose achievements you think should be considered for the exhibition. Say
>
> - who you have chosen and why
> - what aspects of his/her life should be included
> - how the exhibition could best reflect his/her achievements.

Write your **proposal**.

Part 2

Write an answer to **one** of the questions **2–5** in this part. Write your answer in **300–350** words in an appropriate style.

---

2 An international magazine for young people is running a series of articles on wedding celebrations in different parts of the world. You decide to write an article for the magazine in which you describe a typical wedding in your country, and explain what makes such weddings so special and memorable.

Write your **article**.

3 In the film magazine *Take One*, there is a section where readers are invited to send in reviews of very popular films. You wish to contribute by writing about a film you have seen which you think will still be watched for many years to come, explaining why the film will continue to be successful.

Write your **review**.

4 You have recently read an article in your local newspaper about the fact that many people do not use the town library. Write a letter to the newspaper suggesting ways of attracting more people to the library. In the letter you should give possible reasons why people do not use the library. You should include suggestions for improving existing facilities and providing new services.

Write your **letter**. Do not write any postal addresses.

5 Based on your reading of **one** of these books, write on **one** of the following:

(a) Brian Moore: *The Colour of Blood*
Your student magazine is running a feature on political thrillers and has asked readers to send in reviews of books of this type which capture the interest of the reader. You decide to send in a review of *The Colour of Blood* focusing on two episodes in the book, stating why these two are particularly successful in building suspense and maintaining the reader's interest.

Write your **review**.

(b) L.P. Hartley: *The Go-Between*
'Rather than bringing the people of the village together, the cricket match was a reminder that the society of Leo's childhood was still clearly divided by social class.' Write an essay for your tutor considering how far you think this statement is true.

Write your **essay**.

(c) Chinua Achebe: *Things Fall Apart*
Your local reading group wants to study some books set in West Africa. Write a report for the reading group suggesting *Things Fall Apart*. Your report should focus on the way the lives of the people in Umuofia are governed by the beliefs and customs of their clan.

Write your **report**.

PAPER 3 USE OF ENGLISH (1 hour 30 minutes)

Part 1

For questions **1–15**, read the text below and think of the word which best fits each space. Use only **one** word in each space. There is an example at the beginning **(0)**.

Write your answers in CAPITAL LETTERS **on the separate answer sheet.**

Example: | 0 | W | H | O | S | E |

Food for a Future

Jon Wynne-Tyson was an original thinker **(0)**.WHOSE. best-known book 'Food for a Future' was published in 1975. In this classic work, a case was **(1)............** forward for **(2)............** can only be described as a more responsible and humane attitude towards the world's food resources. It had gradually **(3)............** clear to Wynne-Tyson that the economics and ecology of meat production did not **(4)............** sense. What justification was **(5)............** , he argued, for using seven tonnes of cereal to produce one tonne of meat?

Even today, the book's succinct style makes it compulsively readable. **(6)............** his approach is basically an emotional one, Wynne-Tyson goes to great lengths to back **(7)............** every statement with considerable supporting evidence and statistical data. Thus, even **(8)............** of us who are widely read **(9)............** the subject of vegetarianism will gain fresh insights from this book. It is generally agreed that his most skilful achievement is the slow revelation of his main thesis **(10)............** the arguments unfold. The book concludes that a move away from an animal-based diet to **(11)............** which is based on plant sources is inevitable in the long term, in **(12)............** of the fact that there is no sound nutritional, medical or social justification for meat-eating. **(13)............** of whether you agree with **(14)............** a conclusion or not, the book certainly makes **(15)............** fascinating read.

Part 2

For questions **16–25**, read the text below. Use the word given in capitals at the end of some of the lines to form a word that fits in the space in the same line. There is an example at the beginning **(0)**.

Write your answers in CAPITAL LETTERS **on the separate answer sheet**.

Example: | **0** | E | X | I | S | T | E | N | C | E |

The Desire to Know

Curiosity goes back to the dawn of human **(0)**..EXISTENCE.. This irrepressible	**EXIST**
desire to know is not a **(16)**............ of inanimate objects. Nor does it seem to	**CHARACTER**
be attributable to some forms of living organism which, for that very reason, we	
can scarcely bring ourselves to consider alive. A tree, for example, does not	
display **(17)**............ curiosity, nor does a sponge or even an oyster. If chance	**RECOGNISE**
events bring them poison, predators or parasites, they die as **(18)**............ as	**CEREMONIOUS**
they lived.	
Early in the scheme of life, **(19)**............ motion was developed by some	**DEPEND**
organisms. It meant an **(20)**............ advance in their control of the environment.	**ORDINARY**
A moving organism no longer waited in stolid **(21)**............ for food to come its	**RIGID**
way, but went out after it. The individual that hesitated in the **(22)**............ search	**ZEAL**
for food, or that was overly **(23)**............ in its investigation, starved.	**CONSERVE**
As organisms grew more complex, more messages of greater variety were	
received from and about the **(24)**............ environment. At the same time, the	**ROUND**
nervous system, the living instrument that interprets and stores the data	
collected by the sense organs, became **(25)**............ complex.	**INCREASE**

Part 3

For questions **26–31**, think of **one** word only which can be used appropriately in all three sentences. Here is an example **(0)**.

Example:

0 Some of the tourists are hoping to get compensation for the poor state of the hotel, and I think they have a very .... case.

There's no point in trying to wade across the river, the current is far too ....

If you're asking me which of the candidates should get the job, I'm afraid I don't have any .... views either way.

0	S	T	R	O	N	G												

Write **only** the missing word in CAPITAL LETTERS **on the separate answer sheet.**

---

26 When he was in his nineties, the famous writer's health began to ....

If the potato crop were to .... , it would create many problems for the local people.

Please do not .... to check the safety precautions for this device.

27 In the .... term, this new proposal could mean a property tax with substantial rebates for the poor.

Running up the stairs left her .... of breath.

The kids made .... work of the cakes and ice-cream at the party.

28 Sven was the star .... in the school revue with his impersonations of all the teachers.

It'll be my .... to cook a meal for us both next weekend.

Don't drive too fast as you approach the next .... because there's a sharp embankment.

29 When you take into .... the difficulties they faced, you must admit the team did well to come second.

After he had visited the theme park, Trevor gave us a detailed .... of the attractions.

Clara asked the shop assistant to charge the jacket to her ....

30 I thought I had a good solution to the problem, but my plan was .... by the director, who said it would be too expensive.

In many parts of the country, black clouds completely .... out the sun, and whole towns were cast into semi-darkness.

Enrico had to take a different route home because the main road was .... by a lorry which had overturned.

31 When I hesitated over the price, the salesman came up with a special ....

There is a great .... of rubbish at the bottom of the garden.

The two sides tried and failed to come to a ....

Part 4

For questions **32–39**, complete the second sentence so that it has a similar meaning to the first sentence, using the word given. **Do not change the word given**. You must use between **three** and **eight** words, including the word given.

Here is an example **(0)**.

Example:

0 Do you mind if I watch you while you paint?

objection

Do you .... you while you paint?

0	have any objection to my watching

Write **only** the missing words **on the separate answer sheet**.

---

32 Selena really has no idea of the difficulty of finding a parking place.

how

Little does .... find a parking place.

33 The first candidate impressed the interviewers immediately.

made

The first candidate .... the interviewers.

34 I felt relaxed at Gita's house because her parents greeted me so warmly.

ease

Gita's parents .... the warmth of their greeting.

35 The area was completely devoid of vegetation.

whatsoever

There .... the area.

36 No matter what happens, we will never do business with that firm again.

ever

Under .... with that firm again.

37 John concluded that he should take the job.

came

John .... he should take the job.

38 Oskar didn't feel like going out last night.

mood

Oskar .... last night.

39 The news that the Prime Minister had resigned came as a great shock to everyone.

aback

Everyone .... Prime Minister's resignation.

Part 5

For questions **40–44**, read the following texts on motoring. For questions **40–43**, answer with a word or short phrase. You do not need to write complete sentences. For question **44**, write a summary according to the instructions given.

Write your answers to questions **40–44 on the separate answer sheet**.

How noisy do you like a car to be? For me, the quieter the better, but evidently not everyone feels as I do. Recent research in the US and Europe has shown that 80% of motorists like to hear some noises – especially from the engine – as they drive.

Approximately 60% welcomed the blinking of indicators which provide audible as well as visible confirmation that these are working. Other noise sources – among them the horn and the sound of braking – were rated relatively unimportant, as indeed was tyre rumble, which I for one find very surprising. Cars have become so quiet mechanically, and far less prone to create wind noise, that the boom and roar made by tyres running on coarsely-textured road surfaces is now firmly at the top of my list of motoring dislikes. **line 8**

In the aforementioned research, participants were asked to listen to sound samples obtained from a variety of engines running under different conditions. The researchers wanted to know which engine-produced sounds pleased drivers most. The results clearly showed that scientifically measured and subjectively perceived sound qualities are not the same thing. The difficulty facing car designers must be in deciding just how such customer tastes vary according to the kinds of cars they have in mind. The buyer of a top-of-the-range sports car would, they conclude, feel cheated if the powerful engine did not sing like an operatic tenor at moderate speeds, and bellow like a wild animal when the needle neared the red line. Such noises might, I suppose, be anathema to the driver of a luxury saloon car, however. **line 16**

40 In your own words, explain why the writer is annoyed by what he calls 'tyre rumble'. (line 8)

....

41 Explain why 'scientifically measured and subjectively perceived sound qualities are not the same thing'. (line 16)

....

A recent poll set out to discover the top ten driving tunes favoured by motorists. The winner was *Bohemian Rhapsody* by the rock band Queen, which heads a list of similarly rousing numbers from the era of heavy rock music. Such ear-punching anthems have psychologists shaking their heads – not in time to the beat, but in dismay. For this sort of music, they warn, can cause aggressive driving. Armies used to play martial drum beats to stir their troops into battle, and the effect works in traffic too. If you hear pounding music that makes you want to drive forward when all you can see is the back bumper of the car in front, it's quite likely to raise both your blood pressure and your frustration levels. **line 7**

On the open road, fast music is going to make you want to drive faster. It's also going to make you more aggressive, and that's probably going to mean that you're tempted to take more risks. These arguments are supported by earlier research which examined the performance of young people aged between 17 and 25. The report concluded that unsafe drivers in this age group are more likely to go for up-tempo music with a heavy bass.

But that wasn't all. There was also evidence that loud music played in a confined space, such as a car, could have the effect of blanking out that part of the brain that performs logical reasoning.

42 Which word from the text best sums up the scientists' attitude towards the results of the recent poll?

....

43 Which word, used earlier in this text, anticipates the idea which is introduced by the verb 'to stir' in line 7?

....

44 In a paragraph of **50–70** words, summarise **in your own words as far as possible** the various ways in which, according to the research described in **both** texts, different types of sound affect drivers. Write your summary **on the separate answer sheet**.

PAPER 4 LISTENING (40 minutes approximately)

Part 1

You will hear four different extracts. For questions **1–8**, choose the answer (**A**, **B** or **C**) which fits best according to what you hear. There are two questions for each extract.

Extract One

You hear a radio presenter introducing an item on transport.

1 What does the consultation document deal with?

A increased regulation of air traffic control
B difficulties facing the aviation industry
C economies to be made in airport management

	1

2 What is the transport minister's aim when she speaks?

A to predict areas of potential national investment
B to discourage the public from flying so much in future
C to reduce people's expectations of government action

	2

Extract Two

In a radio play, you hear a woman talking about birthdays.

3 How did she react when her husband forgot her birthday?

A She realised that it was of no consequence.
B She became rather depressed.
C She felt slightly disappointed.

	3

4 How does her birthday make her feel these days?

A sentimental
B optimistic
C regretful

	4

Extract Three

You hear a radio discussion about science and technology museums.

5 The man differs from the woman in his opinion of

A the contents of a particular museum.
B the educational value of museums.
C the way museum exhibitions are designed.

	5

6 The woman supports her argument by

A drawing on personal experience.
B supplying a series of examples.
C relying on research evidence.

	6

Extract Four

You hear a reviewer talking about a historical novel which she has read recently.

7 Which aspect of the book does she single out for criticism?

A the accuracy of the historical background
B the style in which it is written
C the writer's attempts at comedy

	7

8 What overall impression of the book does she express?

A It's an insult to her intelligence.
B It shouldn't be taken too seriously.
C It must have been written as a joke.

	8

Part 2

You will hear part of a radio talk about a small mammal called the brown hare. For questions **9–17**, complete the sentences with a word or short phrase.

The brown hare has often provided both [**9**] with ideas for their work.

A fall in the number of hares in Britain is a cause of concern for [**10**]

During the day, hares are often found in areas where [**11**] give protection.

The behaviour known as 'pursuit deterrence' is said to save the [**12**] of hares and foxes alike.

In Britain, hares are easiest to see in the month of [**13**], partly because the days become longer.

Researchers were surprised to find that hares did not seem better off as a result of developments in [**14**]

The population distribution of hares across Britain is described as [**15**]

An organisation called the [**16**] has set up projects aimed at helping hares.

What's referred to as a [**17**] has been produced to try to reverse the fall in hare numbers in Britain.

Part 3

You will hear an interview with a British film director, Ann Howard, who has recently made a film in Hollywood. For questions **18–22**, choose the answer (**A**, **B**, **C** or **D**) which fits best according to what you hear.

---

18 Why did Ann go to work in Hollywood?

A She liked the studio system.
B She needed to work independently.
C Her aim was to make a film about Hollywood.
D Her films were successful.

	18

19 What does she see as the main problem with the film she made in Hollywood?

A It was set in America.
B It was not meant to be a comedy.
C It was rewritten in parts.
D It used American actors.

	19

20 On balance, she found the experience of directing the film

A depressing.
B confusing.
C rewarding.
D fascinating.

	20

21 What is her main criticism of the preview system?

A The audience is made up of film critics.
B The films are not previewed in enough places.
C The audiences go with the wrong attitude.
D The questions asked are not appropriate.

	21

22 She feels that film previews are useful

A as a marketing tool.
B if the director uses the information.
C when the audience pays to see them.
D before films are shown on television.

	22

Part 4

You will hear part of a radio discussion in which two friends, Frieda and Martin, are being interviewed about tidiness. For questions **23–28**, decide whether the opinions are expressed by only one of the speakers, or whether the speakers agree.

Write **F** for Frieda,
M for Martin,
or **B** for Both, where they agree.

---

23 Tidiness was instilled in me as a child. | 23 |

24 The decision to keep things isn't based on their usefulness. | 24 |

25 Parents' attitudes to tidiness influence their children's character. | 25 |

26 Everyone has a different idea of what tidiness is. | 26 |

27 Tidying doesn't get in the way of work. | 27 |

28 A person's appearance is not a reliable indicator of their tidiness. | 28 |

PAPER 5 SPEAKING (19 minutes)

There are two examiners. One (the interlocutor) conducts the test, providing you with the necessary materials and explaining what you have to do. The other examiner (the assessor) will be introduced to you, but then takes no further part in the interaction.

Part 1 (3 minutes)

The interlocutor first asks you and your partner a few questions which focus on information about yourselves and personal opinions.

Part 2 (4 minutes)

In this part of the test you and your partner are asked to talk together. The interlocutor places a set of pictures on the table in front of you. There may be only one picture in the set or as many as seven pictures. This stimulus provides the basis for a discussion. The interlocutor first asks an introductory question which focuses on two of the pictures (or in the case of a single picture, on aspects of the picture). After about a minute, the interlocutor gives you both a decision-making task based on the same set of pictures.

The pictures for Part 2 are on pages C6–C7 of the colour section.

Part 3 (12 minutes)

You are each given the opportunity to talk for two minutes, to comment after your partner has spoken and to take part in a more general discussion.

The interlocutor gives you a card with a question written on it and asks you to talk about it for two minutes. After you have spoken, your partner is first asked to comment and then the interlocutor asks you both another question related to the topic on the card. This procedure is repeated, so that your partner receives a card and speaks for two minutes, you are given an opportunity to comment and a follow-up question is asked.

Finally, the interlocutor asks some further questions, which leads to a discussion on a general theme related to the subjects already covered in Part 3.

The cards for Part 3 are on pages C2 and C10 of the colour section.

Test 4

PAPER 1 READING (1 hour 30 minutes)

Part 1

For questions **1–18**, read the three texts below and decide which answer (**A**, **B**, **C** or **D**) best fits each gap.

Mark your answers **on the separate answer sheet.**

Photography

When a photographer takes a photograph, he or she makes a selection of visual information that is **(1)** .... by his or her technical and aesthetic skills, personal views and experience, together with a **(2)** .... of social and cultural norms. And in the **(3)** .... of this book we shall see how these factors not only affect the style, content and expression of a photograph, but also how those images are perceived and responded to by the viewer. For example, we might consider that the **(4)** .... reader of a newspaper will have an implicit understanding of the photographic images reproduced on the page. But rather than accepting the photograph at face **(5)** .... , we might question whether it accurately recorded the scene as it would have looked at the time. Or, in contrast, does it communicate the photographer's point of view? Is it the **(6)** .... instant recorded that is of particular importance, or should the photograph on the page be understood as a symbol to represent a state of affairs in the world?

1	**A** concluded	**B** imposed	**C** determined	**D** directed
2	**A** group	**B** set	**C** band	**D** batch
3	**A** course	**B** progress	**C** means	**D** process
4	**A** shallow	**B** casual	**C** slight	**D** random
5	**A** regard	**B** esteem	**C** respect	**D** value
6	**A** accurate	**B** definite	**C** precise	**D** absolute

More than a game

Sport for me has always been more than just a game. The most successful people in sport have total self-belief. You need tunnel **(7)** .... if you want to succeed in sport. There's only one route to being the best and you have to put everything else to one **(8)** ..... . Sport is ruthless and no one else is going to do it for you. It's sink or **(9)** ..... .

Sport has taught me personal discipline and determination, but it can also teach you the benefits of working as one of a team. My sport allows and encourages you to **(10)** .... individually, yet it is a team game and you have to balance these two aspects. It's very much like life – you can succeed as an individual, but you must never forget there are others around you.

Sport has given me a great deal – and not just financially. It has opened **(11)** .... for me and opened my eyes, and I've seen things around the world that others will never see. But you also have to give up a lot for those **(12)** ..... .

7	**A** sight	**B** view	**C** vision	**D** outlook
8	**A** margin	**B** side	**C** part	**D** edge
9	**A** swim	**B** float	**C** sail	**D** drift
10	**A** outdo	**B** surpass	**C** outshine	**D** excel
11	**A** gates	**B** doors	**C** windows	**D** barriers
12	**A** supplements	**B** tips	**C** perks	**D** complements

Tuning in

Some experiences **(13)** .... themselves so sharply on our memory that they form islands of clarity in our recollection. For me, such a momentous **(14)** .... took place one night in California many years ago, when I lay awake listening to the rapturous strains of a mockingbird singing from an invisible **(15)** .... in one of the tall trees that were **(16)** .... around the suburban neighbourhood. I don't suffer from insomnia – it was the exquisite artistry of the singer that kept me awake. As I followed his intricately woven melodies, I found myself **(17)** .... into an unexpected aesthetic environment. In order to follow the patterns that issued from the bird, I had to call on my experience of jazz and Indian classical music. The bird had me **(18)** .... that I was being treated to an ad lib performance of the most breathtaking improvisational acrobatics. I groaned and I cheered as one improbable musical variation followed another through the open window where I lay listening, until finally I fell asleep.

13	**A** etch	**B** scratch	**C** trace	**D** cut
14	**A** proceeding	**B** circumstance	**C** development	**D** occasion
15	**A** venue	**B** location	**C** situation	**D** area
16	**A** spotted	**B** dabbed	**C** dotted	**D** flecked
17	**A** engaged	**B** captivated	**C** pushed	**D** drawn
18	**A** prevailed	**B** proved	**C** convinced	**D** confirmed

Part 2

You are going to read four extracts which are all concerned in some way with holidays and travel. For questions **19–26**, choose the answer (**A**, **B**, **C** or **D**) which you think fits best according to the text.

Mark your answers **on the separate answer sheet**.

Holiday reading

Summer promises us two of life's great joys: escaping home and reading books – joys that are, of course, intimately connected. Books may help us to feel more at home in the world at large. We can relate our experiences to those described in great books written long ago or in distant lands because there are fewer human types than there are people. In the books of others, we find our own thoughts, embarrassments and dramas. Authors can locate words to depict a situation we thought ourselves alone in feeling, or can express our very own thoughts, but with a clarity and psychological accuracy we could not match. What was shy and confused within us is unapologetically and cogently phrased in them, a congruence all the more striking if the work was written by someone in a far-flung place or in another age. We feel grateful to these strangers for reminding us of who we are.

Through reading and travel, we escape the deadening effect of habit. Our eyes are never more open than during our first few days in a new place: except perhaps during our reading of a great book, which guides us to the interest of things we had previously ignored. Our mind is like a radar newly attuned to pick up certain objects floating through consciousness. Our attention is drawn to the shades of the sky, to the changeability of a face, to the hypocrisy of a friend, or to a submerged sadness about a situation that we had previously not even known we could feel sad about.

19 What does the author find especially remarkable about great books?

- **A** their uniqueness and creativity
- **B** their timelessness and universality
- **C** their emotion and sentimentality
- **D** their subtlety and complexity

20 What beneficial effect do holidays and books share?

- **A** They heighten people's sensitivity.
- **B** They transport us into a new world.
- **C** They restore balance to people's lives.
- **D** They make people more positive in their outlook.

Author's Note

These travel reflections were all published as articles in the *Observer* newspaper over a seven-year period. Here and there I have restored some small cuts by the editor, which had to be made if the piece was to fit the page, but otherwise I have added very little. The occasional outright howler has been corrected, but only if it was a matter of detail which I should have got right in the first place. Hindsight would have allowed further improvements, but there would have been no end to the process. In the second article about China, for example, it seemed likely at the time, and for some time after, that the Hong Kong dollar would hold up. A year later it fell. If I were to rewrite the piece so as to predict this fact, it would become a claim to prescience, or at any rate no longer a report written at that moment. But like any other flying visitor, in South East Asia or anywhere else, I was there at that moment, ignorant as to what would happen next, and fully occupied with making the most elementary sense of what had happened already. That has been the real story of mass jet travel: the world opening up to people who have no qualifications for exploring it except the price of a ticket. But I have never been able to believe that all my fellow travellers were quite blind. Even a postcard can be written with a purpose.

21 In making his articles suitable for publication in a book, the writer has

A incorporated some comments from his editor.
B shortened some pieces for design reasons.
C combined some shorter extracts.
D changed some factual mistakes.

22 Why did the writer decide against further improvements to the articles?

A He fears any changes might be inaccurate.
B He wanted to retain his original feeling of discovery.
C Changes would have been too difficult to make.
D The differences in style would have been too obvious.

Ecotourism

If there were awards for tourism phrases that have been hijacked, diluted and misused, then 'ecotourism' would earn top prize. The term first surfaced in the early 1980s, reflecting a surge in environmental awareness and a realisation by tour operators that many travellers wanted to believe their presence abroad (line 4) would not have a negative impact. It rapidly became the hottest marketing tag a (line 5) holiday could carry.

These days the ecotourism label has broadened out to cover anything from a two-week tour living with remote tribes, to a one-hour motor boat trip through an Australian gorge. In fact, any tour that involves cultural interaction, natural beauty spots, wildlife or a dash of soft adventure is likely to be included in the (line 10) overflowing ecotourism folder. There is no doubt the original motives behind the movement were honourable attempts to provide a way for those who cared to (line 12) make informed choices, but the lack of regulations and a standard industry definition left many travellers lost in an ecotourism jungle.

23 Which words imply support of certain holidaymakers?

- **A** wanted to believe their presence abroad (line 4)
- **B** became the hottest marketing tag (line 5)
- **C** included in the overflowing ecotourism folder (lines 10–11)
- **D** cared to make informed choices (lines 12–13)

24 In the extract as a whole, what point is the writer making about the term 'ecotourism'?

- **A** It is becoming less acceptable.
- **B** The initial intentions were misguided.
- **C** There is a lot of uncertainty about what it means.
- **D** A more precise term was originally rejected.

Transylvanian Journey

The notebook covering the Transylvanian leg of my journey was lost for 50 years, and only restored a few years ago by a great stroke of luck. It has been a great help to me in reconstructing that period and committing it to print, but not the unfailing prop it should have been. For in Transylvania I found myself having a much easier time of it than I had planned, drifting from one hospitable country house to another, often staying for weeks. When I came to a standstill during those long halts, writing stopped too; as I was keeping a journal of travel, I wrongly thought there was nothing to record. I was often slow to take it up again when I moved on and, even then, jotted notes sometimes took the place of sustained narrative.

Fearing some details might have got out of sequence when I started writing the present book, I surrounded these passages with a cloud of provisos and hedged bets. Then the thought that these pages were not a guidebook persuaded me that it didn't matter very much, so I let the story tell itself free of debilitating caveats.

25 Which of the following statements about the writer's notebook is true?

A It was not a completely reliable account of his journey.
B It was published 50 years after the journey took place.
C Much of the information in it was not relevant.
D The handwriting proved difficult to read.

26 In the second paragraph, what course of action did the writer take?

A He worked on reordering some of the facts in the notebook.
B He stated in the book that some of the facts might not be correct.
C He abandoned his attempt to revise the text of the book.
D He put in anecdotes to enhance the narrative of the book.

Part 3

You are going to read an extract from a short story. Seven paragraphs have been removed from the extract. Choose from the paragraphs **A–H** the one which fits each gap (**27–33**). There is one extra paragraph which you do not need to use.

Mark your answers **on the separate answer sheet.**

Family Business

'Look here, it's no good!' said my Dad. We were in the car on the way back to London. My father, with my brother Maurice in tow, had just collected me and my trunk from the posh girls' school I attended. He had also just sat through Parents' Day, in the course of which I was presented with the Latin prize and the prize for the girl who had done best in her end-of-school exams. He had had a long conversation with my headteacher, and now here we were bound for home and holidays.

27

'So?' I said, brazening it out. 'Mightn't that be useful?'

'I am also given to understand,' he went on, and then I knew the confrontation was coming, 'that you have ambitions to be a barrister. A barrister of all things!' My father knew quite a lot about barristers and the law.

28

'I don't know about that,' I said. 'All I know is what I see in television dramas.'

'Be that as it may,' he went on, pulling himself together, 'I feel your heart's never going to be in the business now. Obviously, you'll go to Oxford University, and after that I can't see you fancying it.'

29

'It's too soon to know,' I said feebly.

'I tell you you're not going to want to join us,' said my father, who had an annoying way of usually being right in such prophecies, 'and it's a pity because you've got the gifts – the brains, the nerves, the vision.'

30

It was not as if my mother was around to lend a hand – she had died early in my childhood and my father had brought me and Maurice up. Maurice was two years younger than I was, and because he was motherless, early in our lives I got into the habit of taking care of him. It was not a hardship. I loved Maurice. Because the business was so successful we lived in a good deal of luxury – in a big house in London, posh schools for both of us, nice clothes, parties, theatres, operas. My father knew all kinds of people – politicians, actors, businessmen – and our house buzzed with good talk and interesting encounters.

31

'OK,' I said, relieved to be spared immediate choices and decisions, and especially the bout of depression and sulks my father would sink into if I opposed him. This was the way he controlled us. So it happened. In my last term at school, and then on vacations from university, I lent a hand, never more than about twice a year, and always on the safer assignments. I became one of the smarter undergraduates, with a little house of my own, a small but powerful white car, designer clothes, and a black dress with a Paris label that I intended to wear when I took my final exams.

32

This was not to be. My father told me that, in about a week, he needed me to do one last assignment for him, that it was the most important piece of business the family firm had ever attempted, and that he would see that it was more than worth my while.

'But Dad,' I protested, 'I've got my final exams coming up, and I just need to concentrate on that. It's really important that I do well and I don't want to have to think about anything else just now.'

33	

That was not all. As he described the procedures I saw more clearly than ever before the single-mindedness of my father – the clarity and resourcefulness with which he set about his life's work, the dynamic energy, the perfect self-control of the man. In his way he was a sort of genius, and I bowed to that in him. It made my own plans and hopes seem less important.

'All right,' I said. 'I'll do it.'

A It was in my last term that my father came up to see me and drove me out to a village for a meal and a chat. There were only a few weeks to go. My tutor predicted I would get a First Class degree (in Law), and I knew that if I kept my head and spent these last precious days carefully arranging information in my mind, he might well be right. I felt poised, confident, concentrated.

B The trouble was that, like most children of hereditary trades, I did feel confined by the family expectations. I could see there were various professions open to me, and I wanted to explore the possibilities. At the same time, like a coward, I didn't want to upset my father. I wasn't as frightened of him as Maurice was – I was the favourite – but I found him formidable.

C 'What isn't?' I said, though I had guessed the trend of his thoughts from my father's unusual silence. He was a talkative man as a rule. 'You can't fool me. You'll do what you want now,' he said. 'What with all those certificates. I was told you will get a scholarship to Oxford.'

D I was studying hard one day when a letter arrived from Maurice. He mentioned that a friend had asked him to join him in setting up a business, that he was really attracted to the idea, but that Father was against it. He wrote that Father was a danger to us both and did not care about us as much as he pretended. He wondered whether now was the time for him to break free of Father.

E 'There's still Maurice,' I said, sullen. My father snorted. We both knew Maurice hated the business. 'Anyway,' I went on, 'you could always use me as a sort of consultant.'

F I could tell that such pressures were simply beyond my father's imagination (or was it that he was somehow jealous of my life away from him?) and that he would interpret a refusal from me as a heartless betrayal in his hour of need.

G 'I just said that,' I said. 'I couldn't think of anything else to say!'

'And apparently,' he went on, 'you have the right sort of personality – you can pick the bones out of a mass of material pretty quickly, you have the gift of the gab and you enjoy performing.'

H 'I tell you what,' my father continued our conversation. 'You can go on helping us out in holidays until you leave Oxford, and then if you decide to leave us you can. It will give you a bit of pocket money, and be a real help to me.'

Part 4

You are going to read an extract from a book about the mind. For questions **34–40**, choose the answer (**A**, **B**, **C** or **D**) which you think fits best according to the text.

Mark your answers **on the separate answer sheet.**

There are some activities that just will not be rushed. They take the time they take. If you are late for a meeting, you can hurry. But if you are impatient with the mayonnaise and add the oil too quickly, it curdles. If you start tugging with frustration on a tangled fishing line, the knot just becomes tighter.

The mind, too, works at different speeds. Some of its functions are performed at lightning speeds; others take seconds, minutes, hours, days or even years to complete their course. Some can be speeded up – we can become quicker at solving crossword puzzles or doing mental arithmetic. But others cannot be rushed, and if they are, then they will break down, like the mayonnaise, or get tangled up, like the fishing line. 'Think fast; we need the results' may sometimes be as absurd a notion, or at least as counterproductive, as the attempt to cram a night's rest into half the time. We learn, think and know in a variety of ways, and these modes of the mind operate at different speeds, and are good for different mental jobs. 'He who hesitates is lost,' says one proverb. 'Look before you leap,' says another. And both are true. line 10

Roughly speaking, the mind possesses three different processing speeds. The first is faster than thought. Some situations demand an unselfconscious, instantaneous reaction. When my motorbike skidded on a wet road in London some years ago, my brain and my body immediately choreographed for me an intricate and effective set of movements that enabled me to keep my seat – and it was only after the action was all over that my conscious mind and my emotions started to catch up. Neither a concert pianist nor an Olympic fencer has time to figure out what to do next. There is a kind of 'intelligence' that works more rapidly than thinking. This mode of fast physical intelligence could be called our 'wits'. (The five senses were originally known as 'the five wits'.)

Then there is thought itself: the sort of intelligence which does involve figuring matters out, weighing up the pros and cons, constructing arguments and solving problems. A mechanic working out why an engine will not fire, a scientist trying to interpret an intriguing experimental result, a student wrestling with an assignment: all are employing a way of knowing that relies on reason and logic, on deliberate conscious thinking. We often call this kind of intelligence 'intellect'. Someone who is good at solving these sorts of problems we call 'bright' or 'clever'.

But below this, there is another mental register that proceeds more slowly still. It is often less purposeful and clear-cut, more playful, leisurely or dreamy. In this mode we are ruminating or mulling things over; being contemplative or meditative. Perched on a seaside rock, lost in the sound and the motion of the surf, or hovering just on the brink of sleep or waking, we are in a different mental mode from the one we find ourselves in as we plan a meal or dictate a letter. This leisurely, apparently aimless, way of knowing and experiencing is just as intelligent as the other, faster ones. Allowing the mind time to meander is not a luxury that can safely be cut back as life or work gets more demanding. On the contrary, thinking slowly is a vital part of the cognitive armoury. line 27
We need the tortoise mind just as much as we need the hare brain.

Some kinds of everyday predicament are better, more effectively approached with a slow mind. Some mysteries can *only* be penetrated with a relaxed, unquesting mental attitude. Recent scientific study shows convincingly that the more patient, less deliberate modes of mind are particularly suited to making sense of situations that are intricate, shadowy or ill defined. Deliberate thinking works well when the problem is easily conceptualised. When we are trying to decide where to spend our holidays, it may well be perfectly obvious what the parameters are. But when we are not sure what needs to be taken into account, or even which questions to pose – or when the issue is too subtle to be captured by the familiar categories of conscious thought – we need recourse to the tortoise mind. If the problem is how best to manage a difficult group of people at work, or whether to give up being a manager completely and retrain as a teacher, we may be better advised to sit and ponder than to search frantically for explanations and solutions. This type of intelligence is associated with what we call creativity, or even 'wisdom'.

Poets have always known the limitations of conscious, deliberate thinking, and have sought to cultivate these slower, mistier ways of knowing. Philosophers have written about the realms of the mind that lie beyond and beneath the conscious intellect. It is only recently, however, that scientists have started to explore directly the slower, less deliberate ways of knowing. The hybrid discipline of 'cognitive science' is revealing that the unconscious realms of the human mind will successfully accomplish a number of unusual, interesting and important tasks *if they are given the time.* They will learn patterns of a degree of subtlety which normal consciousness cannot even see; make sense out of situations that are too complex to analyse; and get to the bottom of certain difficult issues much more successfully than the questing intellect.

34 What point is the writer making when he says 'both are true' (line 10)?

A At least two different approaches to a problem are normally essential.
B No one approach is appropriate for all problems.
C Even contradictory sayings can be equally true.
D Success in problem-solving is determined by speed.

35 The writer mentions the concert pianist and the Olympic fencer to demonstrate that

A exceptional mental and practical skills are evident in different fields.
B there is a mental process which functions faster than conscious thought.
C emotions are not involved in complex physical activity.
D the body functions independently of the mind in stressful situations.

36 The writer believes 'cleverness' is rooted in

A skills acquired through practice.
B the ability to explain the thinking process.
C the power of the subconscious mind.
D the power of rational thought.

37 The writer uses the phrase 'On the contrary' (line 27) to emphasise that a slower mode of thought is

A an alternative approach to managing stress.
B indispensable to our mental apparatus.
C a relaxing way of avoiding problems.
D physically undemanding as a means of escape.

38 The writer implies that deliberate thought copes poorly with

A complex situations.
B any situation involving people.
C trivial daily routines.
D tasks with a strictly imposed time limit.

39 The writer advises that it is better to 'sit and ponder' a career change because this decision

A will have long-lasting implications.
B will have a major effect on other people.
C cannot be based solely on rational thought.
D cannot be made without reviewing one's abilities.

40 In the final paragraph it is clear the writer believes 'slow thinking' enables us to

A gain valuable insight into the past.
B maintain our mental and emotional well-being.
C outperform faster-thinking rivals.
D acquire new insight in a range of disciplines.

PAPER 2 WRITING (2 hours)

Part 1

You **must** answer this question. Write your answer in **300–350** words in an appropriate style.

---

1 You have read the extract below in an international environmental magazine which has asked its readers to contribute articles to a feature, entitled *Crisis, what crisis?*. You decide to write an article responding to the points raised and expressing your own views.

> 'Some scientists have suggested we are facing an uncertain future and a possible global crisis. The way many people live is seriously damaging the environment and we know that some natural resources are rapidly disappearing. Perhaps it is not too late for people to change their lifestyle and their attitudes to prevent further environmental damage.'

Write your **article**.

Part 2

Write an answer to **one** of the questions **2–5** in this part. Write your answer in **300–350** words in an appropriate style.

---

2 You have read a series of articles in an English language newspaper in which different writers describe certain possessions, such as an old watch or a favourite item of clothing, which they would never want to replace. The newspaper has asked readers to write letters about an object of their own which they are equally fond of. Write a letter describing such an object and saying why you want to keep it forever.

Write your **letter**. Do not write any postal addresses.

3 A large old building in your area is to be modernised and used for young people. The council has invited proposals for the future uses of the building. As the representative of your local youth group, you decide to send in a proposal. Your proposal should recommend two main functions for the building and comment on how these would improve life for young people in the area.

Write your **proposal**.

4 You have read an article in an English language magazine entitled *It all worked out well in the end.*

The writer described a difficult situation which ended up by being a positive experience. The magazine has invited readers to send in articles with the same title. You decide to write an article describing a similar experience of your own.

Write your **article**.

5 Based on your reading of **one** of these books, write on **one** of the following:

(a) Brian Moore: *The Colour of Blood*
In an essay for your tutor, you have been asked to choose three locations in *The Colour of Blood* to show how Cardinal Bem's character is revealed in the way he behaves in these places.

Write your **essay**.

(b) L.P. Hartley: *The Go-Between*
Your local newspaper has invited readers to send in reviews of novels about children and childhood. You decide to submit a review of *The Go-Between.* Your review should focus on Leo, and comment on how he relates to the adult world which he encounters during his stay at Brandham Hall.

Write your **review**.

(c) Chinua Achebe: *Things Fall Apart*
Your college library is planning an exhibition entitled *When Different Cultures Meet,* featuring books exploring this theme. Write a report for the librarian on *Things Fall Apart.* You should describe the different cultures, represented by Okonkwo and his people on the one hand, and the missionaries and colonial governors on the other, assessing to what extent they learn to understand each other in the course of the story.

Write your **report**.

PAPER 3 USE OF ENGLISH (1 hour 30 minutes)

Part 1

For questions **1–15**, read the text below and think of the word which best fits each space. Use only **one** word in each space. There is an example at the beginning **(0)**.

Write your answers in CAPITAL LETTERS **on the separate answer sheet**.

Example: | **0** | W | H | I | C | H | | | | | | | | | | | | | |

The Changing English Language

All languages change over a period of time, for reasons **(0)**..WHICH.. are imperfectly understood. Speech is really so integral **(1)**............ form of human activity that it cannot be regarded as an entity **(2)**............ itself. For this reason, it is more exact to say that **(3)**............ generation behaves linguistically in a slightly different manner from **(4)**............ predecessors.

Young people are impatient of **(5)**............ they often consider to be the stilted vocabulary and pronunciation of **(6)**............ elders, and like to show **(7)**............ up-to-date they are by using the latest slang. **(8)**............ , as the years go by, some of that slang becomes standard usage. In any case, people slowly grow far **(9)**............ receptive to linguistic novelties, **(10)**............ that by the time they reach their forties, they decry the slovenly speech of the younger generation.

In this respect, language is a little **(11)**............ fashions in dress. The informal clothes of one generation become the everyday wear of the **(12)**............ . Similarly, just as many young doctors and office workers **(13)**............ out their duties in casual clothes, so expressions which were once confined **(14)**............ slang and familiar conversation are assimilated **(15)**............ their normal vocabulary.

Part 2

For questions **16–25**, read the text below. Use the word given in capitals at the end of some of the lines to form a word that fits in the space in the same line. There is an example at the beginning **(0)**.

Write your answers in CAPITAL LETTERS **on the separate answer sheet.**

Example: **0** | C | E | N | T | R | A | L |

Mount Mulanje

Mount Mulanje in Malawi is the highest mountain in **(0)**..CENTRAL.. Africa, part	**CENTRE**
of a range which comprises no fewer than twenty peaks over 2,500 metres. The	
range is readily **(16)**............ by road and a day's drive allows	**ACCESS**
a **(17)**............ circumnavigation. More energetic visitors, particularly walkers	**LEISURE**
and climbers, are rewarded with an experience that is **(18)**............ .	**FORGET**
Mulanje is a **(19)**............ sight, visible for miles around. The giant slab of rock	**BREATH**
appears to protrude almost vertically from the plain. This impression is borne out	
by the existence of the longest sheer rockface in Africa, demanding for even the	
most skilled **(20)**............ . The explanation for this dramatic geography lies in	**MOUNTAIN**
the rock: a hard granite, very resistant to **(21)**............ , which contrasts with the	**ERODE**
softer rocks of the plains.	
Most visitors remain on the lower, gentler slopes, making use of forest huts for	
overnight accommodation. The trek up the foothills, along clearly defined paths,	
is not overly **(22)**............ but may take up to a week. As the climate cools	**CHALLENGE**
gradually, almost **(23)**............ , with every few metres of altitude	**PERCEPTIBLE**
gained, so the full **(24)**............ of fauna and flora is revealed in all its	**DIVERSE**
(25)............ .	**SPLENDID**

Part 3

For questions **26–31**, think of **one** word only which can be used appropriately in all three sentences. Here is an example **(0)**.

Example:

0 Some of the tourists are hoping to get compensation for the poor state of the hotel, and I think they have a very .... case.

There's no point in trying to wade across the river, the current is far too ....

If you're asking me which of the candidates should get the job, I'm afraid I don't have any .... views either way.

0	S	T	R	O	N	G												

Write **only** the missing word in CAPITAL LETTERS **on the separate answer sheet**.

---

26 The two boys were sent home from school but told to .... back the next morning.

The journalist was asked to .... on what had happened the previous night.

My brother seemed unwilling to .... the damage done to his car to the police.

27 Mr Brown has only recently been elected to the .... of directors.

To my mind, an ironing .... is a very mundane thing to give as a wedding present.

The wood of this tree provides the basic raw material from which various types of .... are manufactured.

28 Many athletes have more .... ability than the current champion; his success is due to his positive attitude and good coaching.

It's only .... to feel embarrassed when you do something stupid.

Honey is a completely .... product with an excellent reputation for boosting the immune system.

29 Yesterday morning, the Prime Minister made his first public .... since the elections.

You should never judge people by their ....

The Winslow family gave every .... of being rich.

30 Once the ship gets out into open sea, the captain will .... a course for the island.

This is a special type of cement that should .... very quickly, and then we'll be able to walk on it.

The new sales manager is determined to .... new targets for the company.

31 My Spanish is not all that .... now as I haven't used it for ages.

The food was so .... that it seemed to be burning my tongue.

The robbers drove off with the police in .... pursuit.

Part 4

For questions **32–39**, complete the second sentence so that it has a similar meaning to the first sentence, using the word given. **Do not change the word given.** You must use between **three** and **eight** words, including the word given.

Here is an example **(0)**.

Example:

0 Do you mind if I watch you while you paint?

objection

Do you .... you while you paint?

0	have any objection to my watching

Write **only** the missing words **on the separate answer sheet.**

---

32 Without the new training programme, Fred would never have made the first team.

it

Had .... the new training programme, Fred would never have made the first team.

33 'It's none of your business what I do with my money!' Dimitra informed her father.

concern

Dimitra informed her father that what she .... of his.

34 I was about to leave the office when Tomasso phoned.

point

I .... when Tomasso phoned.

35 I had only just got into my car when I remembered I hadn't switched off the kitchen light.

sooner

No .... I remembered I hadn't switched off the kitchen light.

36 Denise completely ignored her elder sister's advice.

notice

Denise .... her elder sister's advice.

37 Sally has run away from home before.

time

This is .... away from home.

38 People know more about the books Henri writes than the songs he sings.

better

Henri's .... than as a singer.

39 I have been told that you have been late for work every day this week.

brought

It .... that you have been late for work every day this week.

Part 5

For questions **40–44**, read the following texts on brands. For questions **40–43**, answer with a word or short phrase. You do not need to write complete sentences. For question **44**, write a summary according to the instructions given.

Write your answers to questions **40–44 on the separate answer sheet**.

Brands now dominate our shopping habits, working lives and leisure activities. Corporate logos abound, and this 'brandscape' in which we live is global: walk down a street in any city in the world **line 2** and there will be enough brands to make you feel at home.

The intrusion is not just physical: it is mental and spiritual. Research and surveys repeatedly show that brands generate more trust than any institution. A successful brand offers consistency of quality, a point of certainty in an uncertain world; insecure, we latch on to the familiar and predictable. Brands are no longer simply about the qualities of the product or service they sell, but are promoted as a set of values. Consequently, we use brands and we decode the use of brands to establish the status of others.

Now, as brands take on good causes, they are implicitly bidding to legitimise the corporation as a morally and socially responsible institution. The aim is that the audience will overlook the human exploitation and environmental waste invariably involved in the production of the goods, and believe that the corporation is a good thing. Brands have become a philosophy, and when consumers buy the brand, they buy into the philosophical stance of the corporation.

40 Explain why the writer has invented the word 'brandscape'. (line 2)

....

41 Which verb in the text reveals that we judge people according to the brands they buy?

....

On a Friday afternoon in a huge open-plan office in a customer call centre located in a windy business park, twenty minutes from the nearest shop, there is the subdued murmur of concerned customer service representatives handling confused, demanding, anxious customers. Their patience does not falter. It is hard, emotional labour for all 1,700 representatives and it goes on for eight-hour shifts with half an hour for lunch and two fifteen-minute breaks. It requires them to set aside every aspect of their character except an obliging, cheerful, nothing-is-any-trouble manner. How do you motivate someone to be that patient on what is a very low starting salary? The answer is the brand: if your employees love the brand they'll work much, much harder. **line 4**

Brands in the past decade have shifted from being solely about the relationship between producer and customer to becoming one of the most important tools to manage your workforce. The internal customers are as important an audience for the brand as the external customers – you not only sell the brand to the public, you are also selling it to your workforce, constantly. In this office, desks are decorated with positive thinking slogans; the teams of twelve take all their breaks together and social committees organise riotous evenings out. The goal is to turn every employee into a brand champion, and what the management want now from their workforce is passionate loyalty.

42 What does the pronoun 'It' refer to at the beginning of the sentence in line 4?

....

43 Explain, in your own words, how the function of brands has changed over the past ten years.

....

44 In a paragraph of **50–70** words, summarise **in your own words as far as possible** what **both** texts say about the way in which brands influence our thinking. Write your summary **on the separate answer sheet**.

PAPER 4 LISTENING (40 minutes approximately)

Part 1

You will hear four different extracts. For questions **1–8**, choose the answer (**A**, **B** or **C**) which fits best according to what you hear. There are two questions for each extract.

Extract One

You hear part of a radio interview in which a writer, Jim Burrett, is talking about science fiction.

1 Why, according to Jim Burrett, do critics not consider science fiction to be literature?

A The subjects are often too technical.
B They consider it as a lesser form of writing.
C It fails to explore the complexities of human interaction.

[ ] **1**

2 Jim Burrett explains that his science fiction writing deals with

A ancient and universal themes.
B what is going to happen to the world.
C the effect of technology on humans.

[ ] **2**

Extract Two

You hear part of a radio programme in which an academic is giving a talk on cats.

3 In the speaker's opinion, how did domestic cats become part of human communities?

A Cats chose to live in them.
B Farms offered a useful shelter for cats.
C Cats were introduced onto farms.

[ ] **3**

4 What is the speaker doing when he speaks?

A comparing wild and domestic cats
B describing the impact of cats on society
C giving historical information about cats

[ ] **4**

Extract Three

You hear part of a discussion in which Ian Johnson, a photojournalist, is talking about the problems facing his profession.

5 What, according to Ian, are the prospects for photojournalism?

A The quality of work produced seems to be declining.
B The demand for serious professional work is falling.
C The financial rewards demanded by the young are increasing.

5

6 In what way does Ian think the public attitude to news is changing?

A People don't want to read about disasters any more.
B The public want to get hold of news items instantly.
C Readers get bored of any news story very quickly.

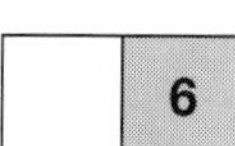

Extract Four

You hear part of a talk on the subject of sound quality in concert halls.

7 What is the speaker involved in?

A managing the finances of a concert hall
B designing venues for musical performances
C recording concerts for classical orchestras

7

8 What is the speaker doing when she speaks?

A describing existing techniques
B suggesting innovative ideas
C comparing rival approaches

8

Part 2

You will hear part of a radio programme about wildlife in which a researcher, Kevin Nelson, talks about a type of duck called the mallard, which he has been studying. For questions **9–17**, complete the sentences with a word or short phrase.

At first, Kevin assumed it was the male duck's

[**9**] that attracted females.

The female ducks are attracted to males whose bills are coloured

[**10**] and have no blemishes.

The ducks find their food on the

[**11**] of the rivers and lakes where they live.

The coloration of the male duck's bill can change according to its

[**12**]

The female ducks are more likely to be attacked by predators in the

[**13**] period.

Amongst the

[**14**] ducks, there is a disproportionate number of males.

Kevin describes the seldom heard call of the male duck as

[**15**] compared to that of the female.

The female duck provides ducklings with both protection and

[**16**] during their first week of life.

Interestingly, when a mother is in

[**17**] she frequently deserts her ducklings.

Part 3

You will hear an interview with Roland Brundy, the new chairman of the television channel GTV. For questions **18–22**, choose the answer (**A**, **B**, **C** or **D**) which fits best according to what you hear.

---

18 According to Roland Brundy, what will be the result of competition within the media?

A a narrower range of programmes on GTV
B the development of new technology
C an increase in GTV's staff numbers
D greater potential for creativity

	18

19 Roland feels that in order to have 'artistic' standing, a channel needs

A an awareness of history.
B to build up expertise.
C accomplished actors.
D to buy expensive programmes.

	19

20 According to Roland, the main problem in reacting to competition is that

A it is hard to avoid copying others.
B all solutions are open to criticism.
C viewers object to change.
D it is hard to interpret the market accurately.

	20

21 How does Roland feel about the impact of technology?

A sceptical
B undecided
C negative
D fearful

	21

22 Roland says that one problem with his type of work is that it is hard to

A adapt to change.
B operate objectively.
C judge its importance.
D measure your success.

	22

Part 4

You will hear part of a radio discussion in which two actors, William and Sonia, talk about their profession. For questions **23–28**, decide whether the opinions are expressed by only one of the speakers, or whether the speakers agree.

Write **W** for William,
S for Sonia,
or **B** for Both, where they agree.

---

23 Learning the lines before rehearsals start is not the priority. | **23**

24 Preparing for a role tends to be demanding. | **24**

25 Good acting depends on interaction with the other actors. | **25**

26 I generally play a character in the same way in every performance of a play. | **26**

27 Actors have more control in plays than in films. | **27**

28 Detail is more significant in films than in plays. | **28**

PAPER 5 SPEAKING (19 minutes)

There are two examiners. One (the interlocutor) conducts the test, providing you with the necessary materials and explaining what you have to do. The other examiner (the assessor) will be introduced to you, but then takes no further part in the interaction.

Part 1 (3 minutes)

The interlocutor first asks you and your partner a few questions which focus on information about yourselves and personal opinions.

Part 2 (4 minutes)

In this part of the test you and your partner are asked to talk together. The interlocutor places a set of pictures on the table in front of you. There may be only one picture in the set or as many as seven pictures. This stimulus provides the basis for a discussion. The interlocutor first asks an introductory question which focuses on two of the pictures (or in the case of a single picture, on aspects of the picture). After about a minute, the interlocutor gives you both a decision-making task based on the same set of pictures.

The pictures for Part 2 are on pages C8–C9 of the colour section.

Part 3 (12 minutes)

You are each given the opportunity to talk for two minutes, to comment after your partner has spoken and to take part in a more general discussion.

The interlocutor gives you a card with a question written on it and asks you to talk about it for two minutes. After you have spoken, your partner is first asked to comment and then the interlocutor asks you both another question related to the topic on the card. This procedure is repeated, so that your partner receives a card and speaks for two minutes, you are given an opportunity to comment and a follow-up question is asked.

Finally, the interlocutor asks some further questions, which leads to a discussion on a general theme related to the subjects already covered in Part 3.

The cards for Part 3 are on pages C2, C10 and C11 of the colour section.

Paper 5 frames

Test 1

Note: In the examination, there will be both an assessor and an interlocutor in the room.

The visual material for Part 2 is on page C3 in the colour section of the Student's Book. The prompt cards for Part 3 are on pages C2 and C10 in the colour section of the Student's Book.

Part 1 (3 minutes)

Interlocutor: Good morning/afternoon/evening. My name is .... and this is my colleague .... And your names are .... ?

Candidates: ....

Interlocutor: Thank you. Could I have your mark sheets, please?

First of all, we'd like to know something about you.

Where are you from, (*Candidate A*)? And you, (*Candidate B*)?

Select a further question for each candidate:

- What do you do?
- How much of your time do you spend studying English?
- When do you expect to finish all your studies?
- Do you live in this area?
- Does it take you long to travel to your work/school/college?

Candidates A & B: ....

Interlocutor: *Select a further question for each candidate:*

- Thinking about where you live, could you tell us something about the people who live in that area?
- Is there anything that makes you proud of the town you live in?
- How good are the entertainment facilities for young people in your area?
- Can you tell us about the things that make you laugh?
- Could you tell us something about your taste in music?
- Thinking about special occasions, how do you prefer to celebrate your birthday?

Candidates A & B: ....

Interlocutor: Thank you. Now, we'd like to ask you what you think about one or two things.

*Select **one** or more questions for each candidate, as appropriate:*

- What languages, apart from English, might be useful to you in the future?
- Some people say that if you're not comfortable using a computer, it'll soon be difficult to find a good job. Do you agree?
- Do you think any kind of letter writing will survive now email is so common?
- If you could change one thing about the place you grew up in, what would it be?
- Thinking about yourself, which do you think creates the strongest memories, sights or sounds?
- How open-minded a person are you? . . . Why do you think this is?

Candidates A & B: ....

Interlocutor: Thank you.

Part 2 (4 minutes) *New website – Promoting cycling*

Interlocutor: Now, in this part of the test you're going to do something together. Here is a picture of a street scene.

Place picture sheet for Test 1 in front of the candidates.

First, I'd like you to look at the picture and talk together about how representative this scene is of life today.

You have about a minute for this, so don't worry if I interrupt you.

Candidates A & B: [*One minute.*]

Interlocutor: Thank you. Now look at the picture again.

I'd like you to imagine that an international cycling organisation is launching a new website to promote cycling. This picture was considered for the website but was rejected.

Talk together about why you think the picture was rejected. Then suggest some other images for the website which would promote cycling more effectively.

You have about three minutes to talk about this.

Candidates A & B: [*Three minutes.*]

Interlocutor: Thank you. *Retrieve picture sheet.*

Part 3 (12 minutes) *Work and money*

Interlocutor: Now, in this part of the test you're each going to talk on your own for about two minutes. You need to listen while your partner is speaking because you'll be asked to comment afterwards.

So, (*Candidate A*), I'm going to give you a card with a question written on it and I'd like you to tell us what you think. There are also some ideas on the card for you to use if you like.

All right? Here is your card, and a copy for you, (*Candidate B*).

Hand over a copy of prompt card 1a to each candidate.

Remember, (*Candidate A*), you have about two minutes to talk before we join in.

[*Allow up to 10 seconds before saying, if necessary:* Would you like to begin now?]

Candidate A: [*Two minutes.*]

Interlocutor: Thank you.

*Select **one** appropriate response question for Candidate B:*

- What do you think?
- Is there anything you would like to add?
- Is there anything you don't agree with?
- How does this differ from your experience?

Candidate B: [*One minute.*]

Interlocutor: *Address **one** of the following follow-up questions to both candidates:*

- What makes a good employer?
- Would you prefer to work for a small family business or an international company? . . . Why?
- What's the ideal size of a work team?

Candidates A & B: [*One minute.*]

Interlocutor: Thank you. *Retrieve cards.*

Now (*Candidate B*), it's your turn to be given a question.

Hand over a copy of prompt card 1b to both candidates.

Here is your card, and a copy for you, (*Candidate A*). Remember, (*Candidate B*), you have about two minutes to tell us what you think, and there are some ideas on the card for you to use if you like. All right?

[*Allow up to 10 seconds before saying, if necessary:* Would you like to begin now?]

Candidate B: [*Two minutes.*]

Interlocutor: Thank you.

*Select **one** appropriate response question for Candidate A:*

- What do you think?
- Is there anything you would like to add?
- Is there anything you don't agree with?
- How does this differ from your experience?

Candidate A: [*One minute.*]

Interlocutor: *Address **one** of the following follow-up questions to both candidates:*

- Would you ever work for little or no pay?
- Would you advise a friend to choose a boring but well-paid job?
- Should people who do dangerous jobs be paid more?

Candidates A & B: [*One minute.*]

Interlocutor: Thank you. *Retrieve cards.*

Interlocutor: Now, to finish the test, we're going to talk about 'work and money' in general.

Address a selection of the following questions to both candidates:

- How easy is it for young people to find employment in your/this country?
- It's often felt that some people are grossly overpaid. Do you agree?
- Would the world be a better place without money?
- Why are certain kinds of jobs disappearing?
- What job skills should children be taught at school?
- At what age should people start earning money? . . . And when should they retire?

Candidates A & B: [*Four minutes.*]

Interlocutor: Thank you. That is the end of the test.

Test 2

Note: In the examination, there will be both an assessor and an interlocutor in the room.

The visual material for Part 2 is on pages C4 and C5 in the colour section of the Student's Book. The prompt cards for Part 3 are on pages C2 and C10 in the colour section of the Student's Book.

Part 1 (3 minutes)

Interlocutor: Good morning/afternoon/evening. My name is .... and this is my colleague .... And your names are .... ?

Candidates: ....

Interlocutor: Thank you. Could I have your mark sheets, please?

First of all, we'd like to know something about you.

Where are you from, (*Candidate A*)? And you, (*Candidate B*)?

Select a further question for each candidate:

- What are you doing at the moment?
- Do you enjoy your work / your studies?
- What's the best thing about the area that you come from?
- How much longer do you think you'll be studying English?
- Do you know what job you'd like to be doing in five years' time?

Candidates A & B: ....

Interlocutor: *Select a further question for each candidate:*

- Do you think your education is/was good preparation for the world of work?
- Can you tell us something about where you're living now? What, if anything, would you like to change about it?
- Could you tell us if there's a particular time of year you especially like?
- What about your hobbies? What's your main interest?
- Are there any sports that you're good at?
- What about food? If you eat out, what kind of restaurants do you prefer?

Candidates A & B: ....

Interlocutor: Thank you. Now, we'd like to ask you what you think about one or two things.

Select one or more questions for each candidate, as appropriate:

- How well can you learn a language without living in the country concerned?
- Thinking about yourself, how representative are you of someone from your country?
- Thinking about computers, how important do you think they are in schools nowadays?
- How important is the place or environment where you study?
- How do you think your chosen area of work will change in the future?
- Do you feel optimistic about the future? . . . Why?

Candidates A & B: ....

Interlocutor: Thank you.

Part 2 (4 minutes) *TV series – Importance of the past*

Interlocutor: Now, in this part of the test you're going to do something together. Here are some pictures which show different aspects of the past.

Place picture sheet for Test 2 in front of the candidates. Select two of the pictures for the candidates to look at.*

First, I'd like you to look at pictures * and * and talk together about what might attract people to these places.

You have about a minute for this, so don't worry if I interrupt you.

Candidates A & B: [*One minute.*]

Interlocutor: Thank you. Now look at all the pictures.

I'd like you to imagine that a series of five television documentaries is being planned to illustrate the importance of the past. Each photograph represents the focus of one programme.

Talk together about these aspects of the past and why they are important. Then decide in which order the programmes should be shown.

You have about three minutes to talk about this.

Candidates A & B: [*Three minutes.*]

Interlocutor: Thank you. *Retrieve picture sheet.*

Part 3 (12 minutes) *Escape*

Interlocutor: Now, in this part of the test you're each going to talk on your own for about two minutes. You need to listen while your partner is speaking because you'll be asked to comment afterwards.

So, (*Candidate A*), I'm going to give you a card with a question written on it and I'd like you to tell us what you think. There are also some ideas on the card for you to use if you like.

All right? Here is your card, and a copy for you, (*Candidate B*).

Hand over a copy of prompt card 2a to each candidate.

Remember, (*Candidate A*), you have about two minutes to talk before we join in.

[*Allow up to 10 seconds before saying, if necessary:* Would you like to begin now?]

Candidate A: [*Two minutes.*]

Interlocutor: Thank you.

*Select **one** appropriate response question for Candidate B:*

- What do you think?
- Is there anything you would like to add?
- Is there anything you don't agree with?
- How does this differ from your experience?

Candidate B: [*One minute.*]

Interlocutor: *Address **one** of the following follow-up questions to both candidates:*

- What are the good things about going on holiday in your own country?
- In what circumstances might people choose not to go on holiday?
- Is it possible for a holiday to be too long?

Candidates A & B: [*One minute.*]

Interlocutor: Thank you. *Retrieve cards.*

Now (*Candidate B*), it's your turn to be given a question.

Hand over a copy of prompt card 2b to each candidate.

Here is your card, and a copy for you, (*Candidate A*). Remember, (*Candidate B*), you have about two minutes to tell us what you think, and there are some ideas on the card for you to use if you like. All right?

[*Allow up to 10 seconds before saying, if necessary:* Would you like to begin now?]

Candidate B: [*Two minutes.*]

Interlocutor: Thank you.

*Select **one** appropriate response question for Candidate A:*

- What do you think?
- Is there anything you would like to add?
- Is there anything you don't agree with?
- How does this differ from your experience?

Candidate A: [*One minute.*]

Interlocutor: *Address **one** of the following follow-up questions to both candidates:*

- As a young child, did you prefer reading books or watching television?
- Should TV programmes for children always be educational as well as entertaining?
- What do magazines offer that books don't?

Candidates A & B: [*One minute.*]

Interlocutor: Thank you. *Retrieve cards.*

Interlocutor: Now, to finish the test, we're going to talk about 'escape' in general.

Address a selection of the following questions to both candidates:

- Where do people go when they want to be alone?
- Why might young people feel the need to leave home?
- What are your strategies for dealing with pressure? . . . Which one works best?
- Some people say that daydreaming is laziness. What do you think?
- Do you think the need to escape from everyday life is getting stronger? . . . Why (not)?
- In monotonous jobs, what sort of rest and recreation should be provided?

Candidates A & B: [*Four minutes.*]

Interlocutor: Thank you. That is the end of the test.

Test 3

Note: In the examination, there will be both an assessor and an interlocutor in the room.

The visual material for Part 2 is on pages C6 and C7 in the colour section of the Student's Book. The prompt cards for Part 3 are on pages C2 and C10 in the colour section of the Student's Book.

Part 1 (3 minutes)

Interlocutor: Good morning/afternoon/evening. My name is .... and this is my colleague .... And your names are .... ?

Candidates: ....

Interlocutor: Thank you. Could I have your mark sheets, please?

First of all, we'd like to know something about you.

Where are you from, (*Candidate A*)? And you, (*Candidate B*)?

Select a further question for each candidate:

- Are you working or studying at the moment?
- What do you particularly like or dislike about the area you come from?
- Have you ever lived in another country?

- Is it easy to travel around your area?
- Have you always lived in the same house or apartment?

Candidates A & B: ....

Interlocutor: *Select a further question for each candidate:*

- Let's think about your free time. What are the entertainment facilities like in your neighbourhood?
- Could you tell us how you like to spend your weekends?
- How important is going to the cinema for you?
- Let's think about your neighbourhood. How easy is it to get to know the people living near you?
- Could you tell us something about the way you've been taught English?
- And what about your plans for the future? Do you have any plans for the near future?

Candidates A & B: ....

Interlocutor: Thank you. Now, we'd like to ask you what you think about one or two things.

Select one or more questions for each candidate, as appropriate:

- How important is it, do you think, to have a hobby?
- What do you most hope to achieve using your language skills?
- Thinking about your education, which teacher (has) made the biggest impression on you?
- Thinking about where you live, how important are your surroundings to you?
- What advice would you give to someone who is thinking of moving to your area?
- Moving on to current affairs, do you keep up with the news? . . . How?

Candidates A & B: ....

Interlocutor: Thank you.

Part 2 (4 minutes) *Calendar promotion – Tourism*

Interlocutor: Now, in this part of the test you're going to do something together. Here are some pictures of one region of Britain.

Place picture sheet for Test 3 in front of the candidates.
Select two of the pictures for the candidates to look at.*

First, I'd like you to look at pictures * and * talk together about why you think the people have chosen to go to these particular places.

You have about a minute for this, so don't worry if I interrupt you.

Candidates
A & B: [*One minute.*]

Interlocutor: Thank you. Now look at all the pictures.

I'd like you to imagine that the tourist board wants to produce a calendar to promote this region.

Talk together about the features that the tourist board should emphasise in order to bring in the most visitors. Then decide which four pictures would be best for the calendar.

You have about three minutes to talk about this.

Candidates
A & B: [*Three minutes.*]

Interlocutor: Thank you. *Retrieve picture sheet.*

Part 3 (12 minutes) *Enjoyment*

Interlocutor: Now, in this part of the test you're going to talk on your own for about two minutes. You need to listen while your partner is speaking because you'll be asked to comment afterwards.

So, (*Candidate A*), I'm going to give you a card with a question written on it and I'd like you to tell us what you think. There are also some ideas on the card for you to use if you like.

All right? Here is your card, and a copy for you, (*Candidate B*).

Hand over a copy of prompt card 3a to each candidate.

Remember, (*Candidate A*), you have about two minutes to talk before we join in.

[*Allow up to 10 seconds before saying, if necessary:* Would you like to begin now?]

Candidate A: [*Two minutes.*]

Interlocutor: Thank you.

*Select **one** appropriate response question for Candidate B:*

- What do you think?
- Is there anything you would like to add?
- Is there anything you don't agree with?
- How does this differ from your experience?

Candidate B: [*One minute.*]

Interlocutor: *Address **one** of the following follow-up questions to both candidates:*

- What makes a book special for you?
- Do you think people enjoyed life more in the past without television or radio?
- What is your favourite newspaper? . . . Why?

Candidates A & B: [*One minute.*]

Interlocutor: Thank you. *Retrieve cards.*

Now (*Candidate B*), it's your turn to be given a question.

Hand over a copy of prompt card 3b to each candidate.

Here is your card, and a copy for you, (*Candidate A*). Remember, (*Candidate B*), you have about two minutes to tell us what you think, and there are some ideas on the card for you to use if you like. All right?

[*Allow up to 10 seconds before saying, if necessary:* Would you like to begin now?]

Candidate B: [*Two minutes.*]

Interlocutor: Thank you.

Select **one** *appropriate response question for Candidate A:*

- What do you think?
- Is there anything you would like to add?
- Is there anything you don't agree with?
- How does this differ from your experience?

Candidate A: [*One minute.*]

Interlocutor: *Address* **one** *of the following follow-up questions to both candidates:*

- How is our enjoyment of city life dependent on money?
- How attractive are cities to children?
- What change to your nearest city would you like to see?

Candidates A & B: [*One minute.*]

Interlocutor: Thank you. *Retrieve cards.*

Interlocutor: Now, to finish the test, we're going to talk about 'enjoyment' in general.

Address a selection of the following questions to both candidates:

- Why do we laugh?
- Can we only enjoy what we're good at?
- What about music and art? What role do they play in our lives?
- How do people help each other to enjoy life?
- How does our enjoyment of life change as we get older?
- Some people choose not to experience new things. Why do you think that is?

Candidates A & B: [*Four minutes.*]

Interlocutor: Thank you. That is the end of the test.

Test 4

Note: In the examination, there will be both an assessor and an interlocutor in the room.

The visual material for Part 2 is on pages C8 and C9 in the colour section of the Student's Book. The prompt cards for Part 3 are on pages C2, C10 and C11 in the colour section of the Student's Book.

This test is also suitable for groups of three students.

Part 1 (3 minutes, or 4 minutes for groups of three)

Interlocutor: Good morning/afternoon/evening. My name is .... and this is my colleague .... And your names are .... ?

Candidates: ....

(......................................)

Interlocutor: Thank you. Could I have your mark sheets, please?

First of all, we'd like to know something about you.

Where are you from, (*Candidate A*)? And you, (*Candidate B*)?

[And you, (*Candidate C*)?]

Select a further question for each candidate:

- Are you working or studying at the moment?
- What do you particularly like or dislike about the area you come from?
- Have you ever lived in another country?
- Does it take you long to travel to work/college every day?
- Which other languages do you speak?

Candidates A, B [& C]: ....

Interlocutor: *Select a further question for each candidate:*

- Can you tell us something about your educational background? . . . What sort of school did you go to?
- What about teachers? Did you have a favourite?
- In your free time, is there a new activity or hobby you'd like to take up?
- How important is sport in your life?
- Could you tell us something about the facilities in your neighbourhood?
- Can you tell us why learning English is important to you?

Candidates A, B [& C]: ....

Interlocutor: Thank you. Now, we'd like to ask you what you think about one or two things.

Select one or more questions for each candidate, as appropriate:

- In your experience, how have the ways in which we learn changed?
- You said you come from . . . . How would you like the transport system there to be improved?
- What kind of environment would you choose to live in?
- Thinking about work, what do you think is more important in a job – money or satisfaction?
- If you could buy one thing to make your life easier, what would it be?
- Moving on to the future – how do you imagine you'll spend your time when you're a retired person?

Candidates A, B [& C]: ....

Interlocutor: Thank you.

Part 2 (4 minutes, or 6 minutes for groups of three)

Book cover – Changing status of women

Interlocutor: Now, in this part of the test you're going to do something together. Here are some pictures of people.

Place picture sheet for Test 4 in front of the candidates. Select two of the pictures for the candidates to look at.*

First, I'd like you to look at pictures * and * and talk together about why the pictures might have been taken.

You have about a minute *(two minutes)* for this, so don't worry if I interrupt you.

Candidates A, B [& C]: [*One minute, or two minutes for groups of three.*]

Interlocutor: Thank you. Now look at all the pictures.

I'd like you to imagine that a publisher is producing a book entitled 'The Changing Status of Women' and wants two images for the front cover.

Talk together about the messages these pictures convey about the changing status of women. Then decide which two pictures would help to sell most copies of the book.

You have about three minutes *(four minutes)* to talk about this.

Candidates A, B [& C]: [*Three minutes, or four minutes for groups of three.*]

Interlocutor: Thank you. *Retrieve picture sheet.*

Part 3 (12 minutes, or 18 minutes for groups of three) *Ability*

Interlocutor: Now, in this part of the test you're each going to talk on your own for about two minutes. You need to listen while your partner is speaking because you'll be asked to comment afterwards.

So, (*Candidate A*), I'm going to give you a card with a question written on it and I'd like you to tell us what you think. There are also some ideas on the card for you to use if you like.

All right? Here is your card, and a copy for you, (*Candidate B [and Candidate C]*).

Hand over a copy of prompt card 4a to each candidate.

Remember, (*Candidate A*), you have about two minutes to talk before we join in.

[*Allow up to 10 seconds before saying, if necessary:* Would you like to begin now?]

Candidate A: [*Two minutes.*]

Interlocutor: Thank you.

Select ***one*** *appropriate response question for Candidate B:*

- What do you think?
- Is there anything you would like to add?
- Is there anything you don't agree with?
- How does this differ from your experience?

Candidate B: [*One minute.*]

Interlocutor: *Address* ***one*** *of the following follow-up questions to both [all three] candidates:*

- Do we expect too much from our leaders?
- Is it possible for leadership to be shared?
- When should leaders retire?

Candidates A, B [& C]: [*One minute.*]

Interlocutor: Thank you. *Retrieve cards.*

Now (*Candidate B*), it's your turn to be given a question.

Hand over a copy of prompt card 4b to each candidate.

Here is your card, and a copy for you, (*Candidate A [and Candidate C]*). Remember, (*Candidate B*), you have about two minutes to tell us what you think, and there are some ideas on the card for you to use if you like. All right?

[*Allow up to 10 seconds before saying, if necessary:* Would you like to begin now?]

Candidate B: [*Two minutes.*]

Interlocutor: Thank you.

*Select **one** appropriate response question for Candidate A [or C if a group of three]:*

- What do you think?
- Is there anything you would like to add?
- Is there anything you don't agree with?
- How does this differ from your experience?

Candidate A [or C]: [*One minute.*]

Interlocutor: *Address **one** of the following follow-up questions to both [all three] candidates:*

- Has learning English made you think more about your own language?
- Do you think minority languages will die out? . . . Why (not)?
- Why do you think children find it easier than adults to learn a foreign language?

Candidates A, B [& C]: [*One minute.*]

Interlocutor: Thank you. *Retrieve cards.*

For pairs of candidates, go directly to the final part of the test on page 127. For groups of three, continue here.

Now (*Candidate* C), it's your turn to be given a question.

Hand over a copy of prompt card 4c to all three candidates.

Here is your card, and a copy for you, (*Candidate A and Candidate B*). Remember, (*Candidate* C), you have about two minutes to tell us what you think, and there are some ideas on the card for you to use if you like. All right?

[*Allow up to 10 seconds before saying, if necessary:* Would you like to begin now?]

Candidate C: [*Two minutes.*]

Interlocutor: Thank you.

*Select **one** appropriate response question for Candidate A:*

- What do you think?
- Is there anything you would like to add?
- Is there anything you don't agree with?
- How does this differ from your experience?

Candidate A: [*One minute.*]

Interlocutor: *Address **one** of the following follow-up questions to all three candidates:*

- What can people do now that they couldn't do in previous generations?
- Is there a particular skill or ability that you admire in other people? . . . (Why?)
- Which of your own abilities or skills do you value most?

Candidates A, B & C: [*One minute.*]

Interlocutor: Thank you. *Retrieve cards.*

Interlocutor: Now, to finish the test, we're going to talk about 'ability' in general.

Address a selection of the following questions to both [all three] candidates:

- Do you think that the media enable us to develop an understanding of other people?
- As we become more international, are we still able to hold on to our own cultures? . . . (How?)
- What abilities do you need to be a good parent?
- What abilities should today's young people be proud of?
- Should people be encouraged to develop their artistic abilities? . . . Why (not)?
- What do we learn about ourselves from competing with others?
- To what extent are skills and abilities disappearing?
- Some people think we are all capable of learning anything. How far do you agree?

Candidates A, B [& C]: [*Four minutes, or six minutes for groups of three.*]

Interlocutor: Thank you. That is the end of the test.

Marks and results

Paper 1 Reading

One mark is given for each correct answer in Part 1; two marks are given for each correct answer in Parts 2–4. The total score is then weighted to 40 marks for the whole Reading paper.

Paper 2 Writing

An impression mark is awarded to each piece of writing using the general mark scheme. Examiners use band descriptors to assess language and task achievement. Each piece of writing is assigned to a band between 0 and 5 and can be awarded one of three performance levels within that band. For example, in Band 4, 4.1 represents weaker performance within Band 4; 4.2 represents typical performance within Band 4; 4.3 represents strong performance within Band 4. Acceptable performance at CPE level is represented by a Band 3. All tasks carry the same maximum mark.

The general impression mark scheme is used in conjunction with a task-specific mark scheme, which focuses on content, range of structures, vocabulary, organisation, register and format and the effect on the target reader of a specific task.

American spelling and usage is acceptable.

Band 5	Outstanding realisation of the task set: • sophisticated use of an extensive range of vocabulary, collocation and expression, entirely appropriate to the task set • effective use of stylistic devices; register and format wholly appropriate • impressive use of a wide range of structures • skilfully organised and coherent • excellent development of topic • minimal error Impresses the reader and has a very positive effect.
Band 4	Good realisation of the task set: • fluent and natural use of a wide range of vocabulary, collocation and expression, successfully meeting the requirements of the task set • good use of stylistic devices; register and format appropriate • competent use of a wide range of structures • well organised and coherent • good development of topic • minor and unobtrusive errors Has a positive effect on the reader.

Band 3	Satisfactory realisation of the task set: • reasonably fluent and natural use of a range of vocabulary and expression, adequate to the task set • evidence of stylistic devices; register and format generally appropriate • adequate range of structures • clearly organised and generally coherent • adequate coverage of topic • some non-impeding errors Achieves the desired effect on the reader.
Band 2	Inadequate attempt at the task set: • limited and/or inaccurate range of vocabulary and expression • little evidence of stylistic devices; some attempt at appropriate register and format • inadequate range of structures • some attempt at organisation, but lacks coherence • inadequate development of topic • a number of errors, which sometimes impede communication Has a negative effect on the reader.
Band 1	Poor attempt at the task set: • severely limited and inaccurate range of vocabulary and expression • no evidence of stylistic devices; little or no attempt at appropriate register and format • lack of structural range • poorly organised, leading to incoherence • little relevance to topic, and/or too short • numerous errors, which distract and often impede communication Has a very negative effect on the reader.
Band 0	Negligible or no attempt at the task set: • incomprehensible due to serious error • totally irrelevant • insufficient language to assess (fewer than 20% of the required number of words – 60) • totally illegible

Paper 2 sample answers and examiner's comments

The following pieces of writing have been selected from students' answers. The samples relate to tasks in Tests 1–4. Explanatory notes have been added to show how the bands have been arrived at. The comments should be read in conjunction with the task-specific mark schemes included in the Keys.

Sample A (Test 1, Question 1)

As we all know sport plays a very important role in people lives. I'm not saying about the international championships or even inter-class competitions but about interesting activity giving us personal satisfaction and opportunity to make a new friends.

This enjoyable aspect is often misunderstood by many people in the world. Many of them are taking up a new sport because of ambition to compete or winning. There's nothing wrong with it, but sometimes we are not able to recognise what's good for us; being too ambitious is disastorous for ourselves and others around us.

My view about a big sport events is not totally clear yet, however, my aim is to put on the spot such event as international championship and to point out what's good or not about it.

First of all mass-media! I think TV, radio and also daily mail are filled up with all this sports informations wchich are acceptable by the major part of the community; by some of peple read with pleasure but for great number seem to be boring. Such information are defenitely a lot more pleasant than the reports about someone's death or plane crash however watching all day long sport's transmisions on TV can be exteremely frustrating.

Secondly; I'd like to ask the question; is the competition between small and big country totally fair? My answer is; Yes it is but on the other hand; bigger countries have a chance to vin more medals as more people is taking a part of the competition. At the same time it doesn't mean that bigger is better.

To sum up it is essential to express my own opinion about sports events. Nowedays sports entertainments are very comercial as most of us see them as an ocassion of earning money and it is somtimes a main reason why young people are taking up a new sport or are forced to do so by their relatives. Isn't it alarming? Young peple must understand that competitive aspect of sport is often misleading. Something what we used to do with pleasure becomes our obsession or the sence of the live. That's why disqualification or being the second is almost always a tragedy for the sports stars.

In my opinion sport shoud be rather a form of spending a free time than competing with others and I hope that the aim of the sport which is good in its nature will convince many of us move into some kind of activity.

Comments

Content
Points covered.

Range
Attempt at a range of expression.

Appropriacy of register and format
Appropriate.

Organisation and cohesion
Superficially follows a structure, but lacks internal cohesion and coherence.

Accuracy
Numerous basic errors which distract and often impede communication.

Target reader
Has a very negative effect.

Band 1

Sample B (Test 2, Question 3)

My town is one of the most beautiful places, so we try to promote it by organizing an annual festival. It is called "Kornaria" and it takes place every summer. This festival commemorates one of the best authors: Vitsentzo Kornaro.

Every June until the first days of September there are many events around different subjects. To begin with, you are given the chance to go to the theatre which is unusual in my area. It may be a dramatic play or one which has a good laugh and sometimes you meet famous people, for examble actors, singers, politicians. Secondly, the festival includes events of historical importance, speeches and seminars are made by expert historians, and exhibitions of local things and products. Besides, night events of folk music and dance are organised which attract lots of local people and tourists. Moreover, (some) other activities of this festival are sports events and painting.

In my opinion, all the above events are important for local life and culture. Local people try to do their best for this festival so they come very close and meet new friends. Also, young people and tourists are informed about our culture, tradition, lifestyle, morals and beliefs. Needless to say that it is financial helpful for my town and many new plans are depended on it. I would like to remark that some people are visiting our area only for that reason.

In conclusion, "Kornaria" is an important factor for our close comunity and still has lots of things to offer (to) everybody. It has been held for more than twenty years and I guess it would be good to retain it. We would be happy to meet you in one of those festivals in the future.

Comments

Content
Points all covered.

Range
Adequate range of structure and vocabulary.

Appropriacy of register and format
Appropriate register and format.

Organisation and cohesion
Attempt at organisation and cohesion.

Accuracy
A number of non-impeding errors.

Target reader
Would be informed about the event.

Band 3

Sample C (Test 3, Question 1)

Proposal

I am proposing that Artur Rubenstein, the Polish-born American pianist, should be included in the 'Great Achievers' exhibition. I have chosen him because, as one of the greatest and more beloved pianists in the world, he made a remarkable impact not only on the world of music but also on the lives of his audiences.

Both his extraordinarily long career – from his teens to his late 80s – and his passionate, genuine love for music and for life distinguish him from the crowd of the great musicians. As a pianist, he is renowned for his unique, magical touch and inspirational power to move, and his perfect interpretation of the works of Chopin led him to be considered the reincarnation of the great composer. As a person, he is famous for his warm, infectious 'joie de vivre', his contributions to the careers of young musicians, and his lively interest in the young state of Israel. When he died at the age of 95, he was mourned for as 'irreplacable', both for his powers as a pianist and the happiness he brought to people from all over the world.

The exhibition should reflect his achievements by including a short biography, photographs and posters of his concerts, and, if possible, a display of his famous inspirational quotations, such as "I have found that if you love life, life will love you back". It should also be noted that he has not always been the legend he is now, and despite his great talent and musical genius, he was not appreciated in his youth. It was through the astonishing determination of practising seventeen hours a day that he achieved such great success and made his music immortal. He has also left an enormous amount of recordings, a sample of which, if possible, should be available to listen to in the exhibition.

Another important part of his life was his contribution to the then newly created state of Israel, which he visited many times and for which he played a great number of charity concerts. Also, the Artur Rubenstein Memorial Piano Competition exists to this day, launching the careers of a new generation of pianists.

Comments

Content
All points fully covered and effectively integrated.

Range
Sophisticated and impressive use of a wide range of structures.

Appropriacy of register and format
Wholly appropriate.

Organisation and cohesion
Skilfully organised and coherent.

Accuracy
Minimal error.

Target reader
Impresses the reader – has a very positive effect.

Band 5

Sample D (Test 3, Question 5a)

The Colour of Blood
By Brian Moore
A gripping political thriller

Brian Moore's "The Colour of Blood" is a compelling and enigmatic tale of mystery and power in which the hero, Cardinal Stephen Bem, tries to prevent an unnamed Eastern bloc country from social unrest and martial law. There is a concordate between the church and the state and Bem has successfully worked for the right to have church schools, to publish religious literature and to worship freely. However, the concordate is jeopardized by right-wing Catholics who are dissatisfied with Bem's politics and try to incite the people to demonstrate against the government.

Bem is detained by right-wing activists, pretending to be Security Police members. One of the best episodes in the book is when Bem manages to escape from his so-called "protective custody" at a checkpoint installed by the army. Immediately before being stopped at the checkpoint, Bem realizes that the alleged Security Policemen are imposters. He manages to get out of the car, but he is then threatened by Colonel Poulnikov who aims a revolver at him. Poulnikov has to hold his revolver in a way that only Bem can see it, but not the soldiers. Bem cannot speak openly to the soldiers as he needs to be free to stop the right-wing Catholics. The suspense is almost unbearable. Bem manages to escape from both parties and the reader wants to know how this is going to end.

Another episode where the reading gets compulsive is the bishop's conference at Bem's residence in Lazienca Street. The right-wing leader Archbishop Krasnov put Bem's authority into question. He reveals having been the writer of the leaflets which urge the people to demonstrate against the government and he denies obeying Bem's orders. Every reader knows that the events at the Rywald ceremony on the following day will be crucial for the future of the country and at the bishop's meeting the ground for a great showdown is prepared. No reader will be able to stop reading at that moment.

Comments

Content
Excellent coverage of the task – two well-chosen events.

Range
Very good use of a wide range of structures and vocabulary.

Appropriacy of register and format
Wholly appropriate.

Organisation and cohesion
Good introduction – well structured.

Accuracy
Minimal error.

Target reader
Impresses the reader – has a very positive effect.

Band 5

Sample E (Test 4, Question 1)

Crisis, what crisis?

It is often suggested that humanity is facing an uncertain future and probably global crisis. One of the main cause of this situation is believed to be the way we live, as such a lifestyle is putting our environment into grave danger. However, it is my opinion that we are actually exaggerating as, frankly, our environment is much better and cleaner that it was a century ago or even two centuries ago.

Lots of scientists argue that the waste that is thrown away seriously damages our eco-system. Tons of rubbish gather in every corner available in the cities therefore being a source of diseases and filthiness. But what they forget is that the situation was even worse the past centuries and that today every country has taken various mesures to minimise the effects. In addition, the number of people who support such mesures has been increasing every year.

Another threat to our environment that is often mentioned is the rate of consumption of natural resources which will invariably lead to their disappearance. It is true that every day we humans "goble up" tons of these resources by means of transport (cars, buses, planes), production (factories), or even every day life (heating etc.). On the other hand, however, other scientists have been trying to find other kinds of resources to keep us into motion such as artificial ones like artificial coal and petrol or natural sources of energy like the sun and wind. In fact some of their researches have been put into practice succesfully.

Furthermore, the majority of poducts that are created are environment friendly as they are made from natural resources. Thus they are biodegradable which means that they can easily be absorbed by the ground without damaging the environment.

All in all, I am cetain that our world is still in good condition and I really believe that we should not panick at all with the warnings of some scientists.

Comments

Content
Valid arguments against the existence of a global crisis.

Range
Good and also ambitious.

Appropriacy of register and format
Appropriate.

Organisation and cohesion
Good.

Accuracy
Minor and unobtrusive errors.

Target reader
Positive effect on the reader.

Band 4

Paper 3 Use of English

One mark is given for each correct answer in questions 1–25.
Two marks are given for each correct answer in questions 26–31.
Up to two marks may be awarded for questions 32–39.
Two marks are given for each correct answer in questions 40–43.

Fourteen marks are available for question 44. Up to four marks may be awarded for content (see test keys for content points) and ten for summary writing skills. The ten marks for summary writing skills are divided into five bands using the summary mark scheme below.

5.2 5.1	Outstanding realisation of the task set: • totally relevant • concise and totally coherent • skilfully organised, with effective use of linking devices • skilfully reworded, where appropriate • minimal non-impeding errors, probably due to ambition Clearly informs and requires virtually no effort on the part of the reader.
4.2 4.1	Good realisation of the task set: • mostly relevant • concise and mostly coherent • well organised, with good use of linking devices • competently reworded, where appropriate • occasional non-impeding errors Informs and requires minimal effort on the part of the reader.
3.2 3.1	Satisfactory realisation of the task set: • generally relevant, with occasional digression • some attempt at concise writing and reasonably coherent • adequately organised, with some appropriate use of linking devices • adequately reworded, where appropriate • some errors, mostly non-impeding Adequately informs, though may require some effort on the part of the reader.
2.2 2.1	Inadequate attempt at the task set: • some irrelevance • little attempt at concise writing, so likely to be over-length and incoherent in places OR too short • some attempt at organisation, but only limited use of appropriate linking devices and may use inappropriate listing or note format • inadequately reworded and/or inappropriate lifting • a number of errors, which sometimes impede communication Partially informs, though requires considerable effort on the part of the reader.
1.2 1.1	Poor attempt at the task set: • considerable irrelevance • no attempt at concise writing, so likely to be seriously over-length and seriously incoherent OR far too short • poorly organised, with little or no use of appropriate linking devices and/or relies on listing or note format • poorly reworded and/or over-reliance on lifting • numerous errors, which distract and impede communication Fails to inform and requires excessive effort on the part of the reader.
0	Negligible or no attempt at the task set: • does not demonstrate summary skills • incomprehensible due to serious error • totally irrelevant • insufficient language to assess (fewer than 10 words) • totally illegible

Paper 3 summary answers and examiner's comments

The following pieces of writing have been selected from students' answers. The samples relate to question 44 in Tests 1–4. Explanatory notes have been added to show how the bands have been arrived at. The comments should be read in conjunction with the summary content points included in the Keys.

Sample A (Test 1)

> The major problem is that any investigation into language origins has to confront is the lack of records that could help us to bring some light to this unknown area. This uncertainty leads to the creation of an enormous number of theories and more on the speculation than on science.

Comments

Content points: (iii)

The summary does not quite cover point (iv), so, although the answer is generally clear and shows effective rewording in places, only one summary point is covered, which limits the grade.

Content: 1 mark

Summary skills: Band 2

Sample B (Test 1)

> It is difficult to investigate the origins of language and there are many speculations about it because, first of all, there are no archaeological records about spoken language as – in contrast with other human activities – it does not have a legible manifestation. The first written records on the issue appeared only long (around 45,000 years) after the birth of language. However, until recently language investigation was not a fashionable target. Plenty of weird theories were made up, serious scholars avoided the question.

Comments

Content points: (i), (ii), (iii), (iv)

This is a good realisation of the task with skilful rewording in places, but occasional errors and awkward linking in places limit it to a Band 4.

Content: 4 marks

Summary skills: Band 4

Sample C (Test 2)

> The new stories are selected by three criteria. Firstly, according to the journalist's intuition about the impact which will have on its readers. Secondly, from the political, financial, social and human importance of the event, and last but not least, the journalist tries to understand if the news will cause excitement to its readers and draw their attention.

Comments

Content points: (i), (ii), (iv)

The summary points are not always clearly made, but there is some attempt at concise writing and the summary is reasonably coherent.

Content: 3 marks

Summary skills: Band 3

Sample D (Test 3)

> Sound influences drivers in different ways. First of all, drivers feel secure when certain sounds confirm their car is working properly. Secondly, sound can please drivers because it fits with the car's image. Additionally, fast and pounding music can lead to aggressive driving, speeding and risk taking. Lastly, loud music can prevent drivers from thinking logically.

Comments

Content points: (i), (ii), (iii), (iv)

The summary is extremely concise, coherent, and strictly controlled. It informs clearly, and requires very little effort from the reader.

Content: 4 marks

Summary skills: Band 5

Sample E (Test 4)

> Brands according to the two texts play a significant role in our shopping habits, in our work and even in our leisure activities. Brands are promoted as a set of values, they are very important in our life. We use brands and we judge people from the brands they buy. In some cases, we see that if the employees love the brand they will work harder. Furthermore, the goal is to turn every employee into a brand champion.

Comments

Content points: (ii), (iv)

The summary is generally relevant and there is an attempt at concise writing. This is, however, offset by some lifting from the text rather than paraphrasing.

Content: 2 marks

Summary skills: Band 3

Paper 4 Listening

One mark is given for each correct answer. The total is weighted to give a mark out of 40 for the paper. In **Part 2** minor spelling errors are allowed, provided that the candidate's intention is clear.

For security reasons, several versions of the Listening paper are used at each administration of the examination. Before grading, the performance of the candidates in each of the versions is compared and marks adjusted to compensate for any imbalance in levels of difficulty.

Paper 5 Speaking

Assessment

Candidates are assessed on their own individual performance and not in relation to each other, according to the following five analytical criteria: grammatical resource, lexical resource, discourse management, pronunciation and interactive communication. These criteria are interpreted at CPE level. Assessment is based on performance in the whole test and is not related to particular parts of the test.

Both examiners assess the candidates. The assessor applies detailed, analytical scales, and the interlocutor applies the global achievement scale, which is based on the analytical scales.

Analytical scales

Grammatical resource

This refers to the accurate application of grammar rules and the effective arrangement of words in utterances. At CPE level a wide range of grammatical forms should be used appropriately and competently. Performance is viewed in terms of the overall effectiveness of the language used.

Lexical resource

This refers to the candidate's ability to use a wide and appropriate range of vocabulary to meet task requirements. At CPE level the tasks require candidates to express precise meanings, attitudes and opinions and to be able to convey abstract ideas. Performance is viewed in terms of the overall effectiveness of the language used.

Discourse management

This refers to the candidate's ability to link utterances together to form coherent monologue and contributions to dialogue. The utterances should be relevant to the tasks and to preceding utterances in the discourse. The discourse produced should be at a level of complexity appropriate to CPE level and the utterances should be arranged logically to develop the themes or arguments required by the tasks. The extent of contributions should be appropriate, i.e. long or short as required at a particular point in the dynamic development of the discourse in order to achieve the task.

Pronunciation

This refers to the candidate's ability to produce easily comprehensible utterances to fulfil the task requirements. At CPE level, acceptable pronunciation should be achieved by the appropriate use of strong and weak syllables, the smooth linking of words and the effective highlighting of information-bearing words. Intonation, which includes the use of a sufficiently wide pitch range, should be used effectively to convey meaning and articulation of individual sounds should be sufficiently clear for words to be understood. Examiners put themselves in the position of the non-EFL specialist and assess the overall impact of the communication and the degree of effort required to understand the candidate.

Interactive communication

This refers to the candidate's ability to take an active part in the development of the discourse, showing sensitivity to turn taking and without undue hesitation. It requires the ability to participate competently in the range of interactive situations in the test and to develop discussions on a range of topics by initiating and responding appropriately. It also refers to the deployment of strategies to maintain and repair interaction at an appropriate level throughout the test so that the tasks can be fulfilled.

Global achievement scale

This scale refers to the candidate's overall effectiveness in dealing with the tasks in the three parts of the CPE Speaking Test.

Marks

Marks for each scale are awarded out of five and are subsequently weighted to produce a final mark out of 40.

Test 1 Key

Paper 1 Reading (1 hour 30 minutes)

Part 1 (one mark for each correct answer)

1 D 2 B 3 C 4 A 5 C 6 B 7 B 8 B 9 D
10 A 11 B 12 C 13 B 14 A 15 D 16 B 17 B
18 A

Part 2 (two marks for each correct answer)

19 C 20 B 21 B 22 C 23 A 24 D 25 B 26 D

Part 3 (two marks for each correct answer)

27 F 28 E 29 H 30 A 31 G 32 D 33 C

Part 4 (two marks for each correct answer)

34 D 35 C 36 A 37 B 38 C 39 D 40 A

Paper 2 Writing (2 hours)

Task-specific mark schemes

Question 1: Sports Competitions

Content
Writer's evaluation/opinion of the following three points on major international sports competitions:

Major points for discussion:
- pursuit of excellence
- opportunities for television companies
- unequal/unfair competition

Further relevant points:
- cost of hosting such events
- investment opportunities for the host nation

Range
Language for evaluating, expressing and supporting opinions.

Appropriacy of register and format
Register consistently appropriate for essay for tutor.

Organisation and cohesion
Clear organisation of ideas with evaluation leading to conclusion.

Target reader
Would understand writer's response to each of the points and conclusions about the value of such events.

Question 2: Humans and Machines

Content
Description of the role of different machines.
Suggestions about possible dangers of dependence on machines.

Range
Language of description, explanation, evaluation and speculation.

Appropriacy of register and format
Register consistently appropriate for article in newspaper.

Organisation and cohesion
Clear organisation and development of ideas.

Target reader
Would understand the writer's view of current situation and possible future effects.

Question 3: Concert Review

Content
Description of the concert and its music. Explanation of why the music was so memorable (explanation may be implicit in description).

Range
Language of description, evaluation and explanation.

Appropriacy of register and format
Register consistently appropriate for music magazine.

Organisation and cohesion
Clearly organised.

Target reader
Would have a clear impression of the concert and its music and the writer's reaction to it.

Question 4: Holiday Resort

Content
Information about the hotel, restaurants and entertainment. Assessment of the suitability of the resort for families.

Range
Language of description and evaluation.

Appropriacy of register and format
Register consistently appropriate for a report. Report format, possibly with headings/subheadings.

Organisation and cohesion
Well-organised report with clear sections and appropriate conclusion.

Target reader
Would be fully informed about the resort and its suitability for families.

Question 5(a): The Accidental Tourist

Content
Description of what is sad in the novel:
- the death of Ethan
- Sarah leaving Macon
- More minor events –
  Macon's accident
  his distress over Edward
  parts of Muriel's life story
  death of Dominick

Description of how humour is reflected in the characters and their actions:
- the accident – as a result of Macon's household arrangements
- Macon's panic attack – Charles trapped in the pantry
- Macon given the wrong crutches in the restaurant
- Macon's attempts to organise his life

(Underlined points must be included. Bulleted points are suggested examples.)

Range
Language of description, narration and explanation.

Appropriacy of register and format
Register consistently appropriate for newspaper article.

Organisation and cohesion
Clearly organised ideas. Appropriate introduction and conclusion.

Target reader
Would have a clear idea of the sad events in the novel and would understand the humorous way some events/characters are presented. Would understand the writer's reactions to these aspects of the book.

Question 5(b): The Colour of Blood

Content
Brief outline of Bem's role at the start of the novel:
- co-operation with the regime – pragmatic approach to the events – reveals Bem's character

description of some of the events Bem is caught up in:
- wife of murdered chauffeur – Bem's concern
- when kidnapped remains calm and clear-headed
- during escape from college – resourceful
- policeman in car, knife sharpener, Jop and his friends – ability to empathise
- undertakes journey to see Urban
- deals effectively with Urban
- takes control once back at the Residence
- at the church – quick thinking

Assessment of how far leadership qualities develop:
- at each turn of the plot, thinks first of others
- rises to the different demands made on him

(Underlined points must be included. Bulleted points are suggested examples.)

Range
Language of description, narration and evaluation.

Appropriacy of register and format
Register consistently appropriate for report for fellow members of book club.

Organisation and cohesion
Clear organisation of ideas, possibly with headings/subheadings. Appropriate conclusion.

Target reader
Would have a clear idea of events in the novel and would understand the writer's assessment of Bem's character / leadership qualities.

Question 5(c): The Go-Between

Content
Description of episodes involving Leo and Marian and those involving Leo and Ted and analysis of the way each treats him and Leo's response to it.
Leo and Marian:
- trip to Norwich to buy clothes
- arranges for Leo to miss boring lunch
- trip to London to buy bike
- plays on Leo's sympathy – Ted going to war

Purpose behind these events and their effect:
- can meet Ted in Norwich
- if Leo misses lunch, he can deliver letter
- bike – will be green to suit Leo's nature
- Leo succumbs – and delivers the last message

Leo and Ted:
- first encounter – Ted patronised by Dennis
- Leo hurts his knee – Ted is kind and sympathetic
- Ted makes clumsy attempts to explain grown-up behaviour to Leo

How Leo was treated by Marian and Ted:
- Marian – apparently totally selfish
- Ted – more hesitation about using Leo; shows more concern for him

(Underlined points must be included. Bulleted points are suggested examples.)

Range
Language of description, narration, analysis and evaluation.

Appropriacy of register and format
Register consistently appropriate for essay for tutor.

Organisation and cohesion
Clear organisation of ideas. Appropriate conclusion.

Target reader
Would have a clear idea of the ways Marian and Ted treated Leo. Would understand the writer's views about their treatment of him.

Paper 3 Use of English (1 hour 30 minutes)

Part 1 (one mark for each correct answer)

1 with **2** no **3** of **4** times **5** then / so **6** addition
7 which **8** to **9** when **10** there **11** by **12** its **13** did
14 what **15** fewer (NOT less)

Part 2 (one mark for each correct answer)

16 rhythmically **17** perception(s) **18** consciousness **19** (un)arguably
20 controversial **21** researchers **22** conviction **23** underestimated
(NOT overestimated) **24** decisive **25** coherent

Part 3 (two marks for each correct answer)

26 power **27** weak **28** position **29** illustrated **30** wings
31 round

Part 4 (one mark for each correct answer)

32 has (always) dedicated **herself** (1) + to her work/job in (1)
33 **come** up with (1) + a/the solution / an/the answer / (the/some) answers/solutions (1)
34 to Henrik's **delight** / to the **delight** of Henrik (1) + he was selected (1) (correct use of apostrophe essential)
35 want to **leave** (1) + anything to chance (1)
36 **purpose** in (1) + calling a/the meeting was (1)
37 as/though it seems/appears (1) + the composer **lacks** any (1)
38 never **occurred** to me (1) + to ask (1)
39 how **hard** (1) + I tried (1)
NB: the mark scheme for Part 4 may be expanded with other appropriate answers.

Part 5 (questions 40–43 two marks for each correct answer)

40 (as) absurd claims mushroomed. No further additions.
41 (the) origin of language. Allow clear paraphrase, e.g. the beginnings of language.
42 Explanation of 'language is our medium', e.g. language is essential to humans / language is important to us / we use language (all the time) / language differentiates humans from animals AND explanation of 'how it evolved remains . . . speculative', e.g. we don't know how it began / its origin. Both essential for the mark.
43 Explanation of 'linguistic competence' e.g. ability to speak / using language / development of language NOT just 'communicate' AND explanation of 'capacity for (complex) thought', e.g. ability to think / formulate ideas. NB: both paraphrases essential for mark.
44 Award up to four marks for content. The paragraph should include the following points:
  i Written records are quite recent / only 5,000 years old (whereas speech is at least 100,000 years old). ALLOW answers like 'there are no written records of the beginnings of language'.

ii Not regarded as a serious area of study / shunned by serious scholars.
iii Large numbers of (absurd/crazy/crackpot) theories AND/OR lack of agreement/controversy (about origins of language).
iv No archaeological/physical/visible record/evidence of spoken language. Not just 'there are no records'.

Paper 4 Listening (40 minutes approximately)

Part 1 (one mark for each correct answer)

1 B 2 C 3 B 4 A 5 A 6 B 7 A 8 B

Part 2 (one mark for each correct answer)

9 P/polar I/institute **10** population disturbance **11** stress (level(s)) / level(s) of stress **12** false egg **13** capture/catch **14** (special) paint **15** fifteen/15 **16** still **17** tour operators/companies/organisers

Part 3 (one mark for each correct answer)

18 B **19** C **20** A **21** A **22** D

Part 4 (one mark for each correct answer)

23 B **24** W **25** L **26** L **27** W **28** L

Transcript

Cambridge Certificate of Proficiency in English Listening Test. Test 1.

I'm going to give you the instructions for this test.

I'll introduce each part of the test and give you time to look at the questions.

At the start of each piece you'll hear this sound:

tone

You'll hear each piece twice.

Remember, while you're listening, write your answers on the question paper.

You'll have five minutes at the end of the test to copy your answers onto the separate answer sheet.

There will now be a pause. Please ask any questions now, because you must not speak during the test.

[pause]

PART 1

Now open your question paper and look at Part One.

[pause]

You'll hear four different extracts. For questions 1 to 8, choose the answer (A, B or C) which fits best according to what you hear. There are two questions for each extract.

Extract 1

[pause]

tone

The relationship of the media to climbing is quite interesting nowadays. It seems that whenever you hear anything in the media about mountains, it's usually tragic; it's usually cost the country thousands of dollars or pounds for a rescue or something. So the general public's perception about climbing is of a bunch of mad people who go literally throwing themselves up and down mountains at the taxpayers' expense. Interestingly, journalists don't write the same type of story about sports people getting injured on the rugby or hockey pitch. Yet despite that, more and more people are getting involved in dangerous sports like mountaineering and, I believe, this is because risk has been largely taken out of our ordinary lives. There's obviously something in the human condition that does actually thrive in a different sort of atmosphere. Our governments go out of their way to make everything we do safer and safer and more and more regulated and, really, I think it's empowering, that's what it is, for people to actually get that responsibility for their own lives back again.

[pause]

tone

[The recording is repeated.]

[pause]

Extract 2

[pause]

tone

A major worry for parents who come to see me is that, as their children progress through school, they become experts on areas their parents know absolutely nothing about! But in fact, it's essential for parents to realise that, in the course of daily conversation with their offspring, they regularly pass on words of wisdom which are crucial to a child's understanding and acceptance of the norms of society. Parents often say their youngsters take no notice of what they tell them, but our surveys of young teenagers show that they have excellent recall of parental advice, and even, in most cases, a quite surprising degree of respect for what we might call their elders and betters.

Of course, the dreaded homework issue often rears its ugly head! To help or not to help is the dilemma, and there's no easy answer to this. Showing interest in a child's school work is one thing, but dictating answers is quite another. Allowing the child to talk through a problem task is usually a constructive way of giving support, but one should definitely draw the line at taking over.

[pause]

tone

[The recording is repeated.]

[pause]

Extract 3

[pause]

tone

Presenter: Self-deception, like hope, springs eternal. Indeed, according to a recent article by the Brazilian social scientist Ricardo Benetti, wherever there is human subjectivity, there are people believing their own lies. For over 2000 years philosophers have remarked upon this, but only in terms of moral opprobrium. Now Benetti is arguing for a more sophisticated response to an endlessly sophisticated phenomenon. I rang him in Sao Paulo, and asked him what he meant by self-deception.

Benetti: It's particularly human. It's related to language and to one part of the mind lying to or manipulating the other part. Traditional logic cannot handle this type of situation. One simple example – you're always late, so you advance your watch half an hour in order to be more punctual, OK? There's a tricky thing going on here, because if, every time you look at your watch, you remember you changed it, it won't work. So you've got to forget what you've done, in order for the self-deception to work. But then you can't remember to forget, because that's a contradiction. You've got to forget you're forgetting about it, and then it'll work!

[pause]

tone

[The recording is repeated.]

[pause]

Extract 4

[pause]

tone

The increasingly meagre amount of airtime offered to classical music on television is a clear indication of its increasing decline in stature. One recent television documentary on the richness of the Renaissance period of cultural history suggested that music was not really part of the overall picture, but a bit-part in the central drama starring the visual arts and architecture. This is an assessment very much in keeping with our time. But we musicians are also to blame. We assume a slow shot of some musicians in dinner jackets ploughing through a 30-minute romantic piece of nonsense, or an egghead lecturing in a dusty concert hall foyer, is enough to grab viewers. Patently, it isn't. The need is very obviously for more programmes about music.

[pause]

tone

[The recording is repeated.]

[pause]

That's the end of Part One.

Now turn to Part Two.

[pause]

PART 2

You will hear part of a radio programme about penguins – birds which live in Antarctica. For questions 9 to 17, complete the sentences with a word or short phrase.

You now have forty-five seconds in which to look at Part Two.

[pause]

tone

Interviewer: These days, even places as inaccessible as the Antarctic are becoming popular tourist destinations. This evening we hear from Amanda Newark, who's been looking into how this may be affecting the local wildlife.

Amanda Newark: My particular study project, carried out on behalf of the Polar Institute, has been looking at penguins. Each year, around 7,000 tourists visit the Antarctic, and one of the things it's possible for them to see at fairly close quarters are the penguins. And conservationists have questioned whether this human presence might be having an adverse effect on the birds. Although there's no evidence that total penguin numbers are declining in Antarctica, we have found some signs of what we call 'population disturbance'.

In our latest study, we set out to investigate penguins while they were nesting. In particular, we wanted to see what effect the proximity of humans had on them. The way that we decided to measure this was to take readings of the birds' heart rate, when the humans were there and when they weren't. Heart rate is a well-known indicator of stress levels in birds as well as in people. The problem we had was how to do this without traumatising the penguins in the process and so increasing their heart rate anyway.

What we had to do was place something close to the bird which would be accepted, and the most obvious thing to try was a false egg, inside of which we could put an infra-red sensor, very similar to that which sports people might use to measure their heart rate. Fortunately, it's easy to get this into the nest. My experience was that, when I approached, the penguin would take one or two steps off the nest, I'd just put the thing in and go away, and then the penguin would get back onto its nest as if nothing had happened. So for this experiment, you don't have to capture the bird, which is good. Despite outward appearances, it might, of course, still have felt very threatened, but that's what we needed to measure. The very nice aspect to this project is that I was working on a species where the parents swap incubation duty about every twenty-four hours. So I marked the penguin very lightly on the breast, using special paint. This meant that when I came back the next day and had an unmarked penguin sitting there, I was measuring the heart rate of a bird which was completely unaware of my experimental procedure. There was therefore no chance that its heart rate response to humans could have been affected by anything I'd done.

This allowed me to do a number of experiments involving around ten groups of three to five people and then a further series using twelve groups of over fifteen people. And what I found is that with the small groups, there was no increase in the heartbeat when the people were nearby. We can conclude, therefore, that they do not perceive such groups as a threat. The larger groups are more likely to produce a response, but this seems to be very heavily concentrated during the period when the penguins are being approached. So if you have a large group of people moving towards nesting penguins, during that time you do on occasion get very large heart rate increases. But once the people keep still, even though they're close by, then the penguin's heart rate returns to normal.

It's quite good news really, because we often hear about the human effects on the environment, but as far as we can see, the tourists are not having any deleterious effects on penguins. And, of course, it's certainly possible for a tourist group visit to be conducted so that it remains at a safe distance from the nesting penguins anyway. I think the situation is quite positive in the Antarctic, because the tour operators themselves have already shown very great commitment towards good behaviour and towards minimising the effect their clients have while they're ashore.

[pause]

Now you'll hear Part Two again.

tone

[The recording is repeated.]

[pause]

That's the end of Part Two.

Now turn to Part Three.

[pause]

PART 3

You will hear the owner of a very unusual house and his architect talking to a visitor to the house. For questions 18 to 22, choose the answer (A, B, C or D) which fits best according to what you hear.

You now have one minute in which to look at Part Three.

[pause]

tone

Interviewer: This is an incredible place, this tall square tower which you've converted into a house. What was it originally built as?

Owner: Well, in fact, as you can probably imagine from its shape, it was built as a sort of look-out tower. I mean, it was built as a means of defence. Its position is perfect with the river down there.

Interviewer: And why did you want to live in a tower house?

Owner: I think my idea was that having lived for so long in London, travelled a lot throughout Britain, I'm often appalled at the standard of architecture from the middle of the twentieth century, although I think it's improving. I think there's very little one sees where future generations will look back on my generation and will say to themselves that we can see things of great beauty. But I think that what Michael, my architect, has recreated here for me is a very beautiful building.

Interviewer: So Michael, this must have been a dream-come-true project for you, something, I mean, which, well, you must have been thinking about.

Architect: I've always been fascinated by ancient buildings, ever since I was a child, and what we've got here is a vaulted kitchen and dining room, the great hall, a library above that and five smallish bedrooms up top.

Interviewer: And it's not as big as it actually looks from the outside?

Owner: No it's not, it's not large at all, but you're forever carting stuff from top to bottom and vice versa, which can be exhausting sometimes.

Interviewer: Why does the wall sort of belly out a little bit there, at the bottom?

Architect: Well, the reason that happens, well, it's really only in the last hundred years that we've built what we call foundations. Before that, being good economically-minded folk, they took any very big boulders which happened to be there, dug a very shallow trench, and scooped the boulders into the trench, and of course, some of the big stones would be above ground level and that's what gives you this lovely soft junction between the wall and the ground.

Owner: And as we look up, my wife insisted that these, er, windows – there's 42 windows in the tower here – that the windows were double-glazed. Well, obviously, Michael's concern was that the windows weren't double-glazed in the sixteenth century, and they wouldn't look terribly authentic.

Architect: Yeah, yeah. Because this is all authentic vaulting. Buildings like this always had vaulted ground floors, this is the . . . look . . . the arch, makes it look like a dungeon but the ground floor was vaulted, built with these arches, for two reasons: it made it very, very strong and this is really where they held their stores. Eh, it was only latterly that we've extended down and turned them into dining rooms and kitchens.

Interviewer: Yes, as you've done here. And how do you feel now the project's finished?

Architect: Well, I would hope in a hundred years' or two hundred years' time people who are either living in here, or who come to visit the tower, er, might say, 'How very nice, I wonder who did this marvellous renovation in the twentieth century?' Even if I have just altered someone else's original design, I consider it my creation. We've given this building a new lease of life. And who knows what purposes architects of the future may find for it? But I'm sure it will stand for many years to come. It's my place in history, so if someone feels they want to leave something of some beauty behind, I'd say, 'Go for it.'

[pause]

Now you'll hear Part Three again.

tone

[The recording is repeated.]

[pause]

That's the end of Part Three.

Now turn to Part Four.

[pause]

PART 4

You will hear part of a radio discussion between two people, Louisa and William, who have been to a new modern art museum. For questions 23 to 28, decide whether the opinions are expressed by only one of the speakers, or whether the speakers agree. Write L for Louisa, W for William, or B for both, where they agree.

You now have thirty seconds in which to look at Part Four.

[pause]

tone

William: Now, we've both been to the new Northern Museum of Modern Art. So, what were your impressions?

Louisa: Well, it's certainly a bizarre-looking building; it reminded me of a huge garden shed.

William: What did you think of the exhibitions themselves? I found the layout somewhat confusing.

Louisa: But maybe they haven't got their signs quite sorted out yet. It's early days after all. I must say I was surprised by the title of the main exhibition – 'Wounds'. I thought art was supposed to be all about healing nowadays.

William: Yes, but isn't art about how things are? Surely contemporary art is often made, um, usually made, at points of social, either social or personal friction, disruption and anguish.

Louisa: It says in the catalogue, 'the best modern art cuts through the smooth but comforting surface of traditional culture: it's often disquieting, it makes its rules as it goes along'. But I don't think art should always shock, do you?

William: Hmm. But not all shocks are unpleasant, are they? For example, I heard a father say to his children in the museum, 'Come and see this. It's the most realistic sculpture you'll ever see!'

Louisa: Oh, that must have been that living sculpture of seven girls standing at the entrance. That was fascinating. Listening to some of the outraged comments like 'That's not art! How dare they put that there!' made me think they've got a point.

William: It was certainly attracting an audience. People weren't sure if it was a sculpture or real girls posing. It was interesting watching them trying to decide! I think there is a place for this in an art gallery because that's what it is. Anyway, even negative reactions are very healthy. Art needs that sort of reaction to survive.

Louisa: If it *is* art, then that's true.

William: Something that occurred to me actually . . . I just wondered whether the exhibition is a shade ostentatious.

Louisa: There's certainly a lot of spectacle in it, but there are some great pieces and a variety of tempo. You can have your quieter moments like those flickering photographs of paper arrows blowing in the air and the sounds to go with it – very relaxing. Art doesn't have to kind of grab you by the throat to be good, does it?

William: Well, I don't know about that. Anyway, we haven't discussed the regional exhibition yet. I have to say I'm dubious about everyone's obsession with regional characteristics, this idea that in south west England, for example, there's a different light which creates a unique painting style . . .

[pause]

Now you'll hear Part Four again.

tone

[The recording is repeated.]

[pause]

That's the end of Part Four.

There will now be a pause of five minutes for you to copy your answers onto the separate answer sheet. Be sure to follow the numbering of all the questions.

Note: Stop/Pause the recording here and time five minutes. In the exam candidates will be reminded when there is **one** minute remaining.

[pause]

That's the end of the test. Please stop now. Your supervisor will now collect all the question papers and answer sheets.

Test 2 Key

Paper 1 Reading (1 hour 30 minutes)

Part 1 (one mark for each correct answer)

1 B 2 C 3 A 4 A 5 D 6 C 7 C 8 A 9 D
10 D 11 B 12 C 13 D 14 C 15 A 16 B 17 C
18 A

Part 2 (two marks for each correct answer)

19 B 20 C 21 D 22 A 23 C 24 A 25 D 26 B

Part 3 (two marks for each correct answer)

27 G 28 E 29 F 30 A 31 H 32 B 33 D

Part 4 (two marks for each correct answer)

34 B 35 A 36 D 37 D 38 C 39 A 40 B

Paper 2 Writing (2 hours)

Task-specific mark schemes

Question 1: Town Redevelopment

Content
Writer's evaluation of the advantages of each of the following suggestions:

- leisure centre
- hotel
- supermarket

Reasons for choice of **one** of these.

Range
Language of description, evaluation, comparison and justification.

Appropriacy of register and format
Proposal format, possibly with headings/subheadings.
Register consistent and appropriate for formal proposal.

Organisation and cohesion
Clear introduction – to state purpose of proposal.
Well-structured evaluation.
Clear conclusion/recommendation.

Target reader
Would understand writer's opinion of each suggestion and the reasons for the choice of one of them.

Question 2: Musical Memories

Content
Article must refer to a piece of music, describe the occasion remembered and the importance of the occasion.

Range
Language of description, narration and explanation.

Appropriacy of register and format
Register consistently appropriate for magazine article.

Organisation and cohesion
Clearly organised.
Description/narration leading to explanation.

Target reader
Would understand the connection between the music and the occasion and understand the writer's feelings about the occasion.

Question 3: Festival Review

Content
Description of event and explanation of its significance.

Range
Language of description and explanation.

Appropriacy of register and format
Register consistently appropriate for a magazine review.

Organisation and cohesion
Clear organisation of ideas.
Description leading to explanation.

Target reader
Would understand what happens at the event and its local significance.

Question 4: Being Young

Content
Description of writer's experiences of life as a young person or as an observer of young people. Opinion on the headline and reasons for this view.

Range
Language of description, narration and explanation.

Appropriacy of register and format
Register consistently appropriate for letter to magazine.

Organisation and cohesion
Early reference to headline / reason for writing.
Clearly organised, moving from description to explanation and suitable conclusion.

Target reader
Would have a clear idea of the writer's experiences and understand the writer's point of view.

Question 5(a): The Accidental Tourist

Content

Description of Macon's character revealed by:
- the types of books he writes
- his fondness for method in household arrangements
- his pleasure at being 'unconnected' when no one knows where he is
- the fact he reads the same book on every flight

An account of his misfortunes:
- Sarah leaving him
- his problems with Edward
- breaking his leg
- his panic attack

An explanation about how events bring about change:
- Edward's training – his observation of Muriel's method and attitudes
- getting used to Muriel's disorganised household
- his reliance on Sarah in Paris – the final realisation he needs to take control

(Underlined points must be included. Bulleted points are suggested examples.)

Range

Language of description, narration and explanation.

Appropriacy of register and format

Register consistently appropriate for review in an English-language newspaper.

Organisation and cohesion

Clear development of ideas, description leading to explanation and appropriate conclusion.

Target reader

Would have a clear idea of Macon's character, the change in him and the reasons for this.

Question 5(b): The Colour of Blood

Content

Description of what happens in the church:
- when Bem arrives, Prisbek tries to give an incapacitating injection
- Bem escapes into the body of the church
- drama intensifies with the arrival of Urban
- Archbishop tries to address the congregation
- Bem gets to the microphone first
- Bem makes his plea for restraint/peace
- Bem shot

Bem's feelings and the reasons for them:
- his aim has been achieved
- there will be no uprising
- church and state will continue to compromise
- joy that peace will be the end result

(Underlined points must be included. Bulleted points are suggested examples.)

Range
Language of description, narration and analysis.

Appropriacy of register and format
Register consistently appropriate for essay for tutor.

Organisation and cohesion
Clear organisation of ideas.
Account of events.

Target reader
Would understand what Cardinal Bem has been striving to achieve and his feelings when his aims are realised.

Question 5(c): The Go-Between

Content
Description of events that are influenced by the weather:
- Leo's unsuitable clothes lead to Norwich trip
- heatwave – means there are picnics, swimming, Leo's visits to the farm
- storm – on Leo's birthday – carriage is sent for Marian

Explanation of how these contribute to the course of events:
- visit to Norwich – Marian meets Ted
- swimming trip to river – Leo meets Ted – becomes messenger
- storm – everything has built up to this climax: (for Leo, his birthday; for Marian and Ted, discovery; for Ted, death)

(Underlined points must be included. Bulleted points are suggested examples.)

Range
Language of description, narration and analysis.

Appropriacy of register and format
Register consistently appropriate for newspaper article.

Organisation and cohesion
Clear organisation of ideas.
Description leading to analysis.

Target reader
Would understand the crucial events of the story and see how these were influenced by the weather.

Paper 3 Use of English (1 hour 30 minutes)

Part 1 (one mark for each correct answer)

1 no **2** with **3** has **4** but **5** by **6** to
7 (al)though/while/whilst/whereas **8** as **9** goes **10** that
11 so **12** one **13** having **14** what **15** of

Part 2 (one mark for each correct answer)

16 conversant **17** depth **18** inclusion **19** increasingly
20 powerless **21** confidently **22** awareness **23** intricate
24 inability **25** unconnected

Part 3 (two marks for each correct answer)

26 process **27** meet **28** move **29** scene **30** hand **31** image

Part 4 (two marks for each correct answer)

32 in the **light** (1) + of (the) new (1)
33 a **sharp** rise/increase (1) + in the cost/price of (1)
34 waited **for** John to finish eating / his meal (1) + before (1)
35 yourself be/get (1) + **taken** in by (1)
36 (that) there is/are **no** dramatic (1) + change(s) in/to (1)
37 to come (1) + to **terms** with (1)
38 **has** (got) no intention (1) + of (ever) visiting (1)
39 was led/given (1) + to **believe** (that) (1)
NB: the mark scheme for Part 4 may be expanded with other appropriate answers.

Part 5 (questions 40–43 two marks for each correct answer)

40 Paradox in line 1: the contrast between high tech (production of newspapers) and there being nothing scientific about it (the way journalists operate, i.e. by instinct). Both parts of paradox essential.
41 (And where space is tight) news from far away is always the loser. No further additions.
42 (the) lies and trash (of which the tabloids are often accused) AND (a series of [almost]) random reactions to random events. NOT artificial human invention.
43 Paragraph 3 sentence 1: paraphrase of 'judgements' AND 'phrasing' e.g. content and style; comments and way he/she uses language.
44 Award up to four marks for content. The paragraph should include the following points:
- i Guided by feel/hunch/gut instinct/assumptions AND/OR Personal experience/social status/personal beliefs.
- ii News is about the exceptional AND/OR must interest/excite/entertain the reader.
- iii What fits/space is tight.
- iv Political/social/economic/human significance.

Paper 4 Listening (40 minutes approximately)

Part 1 (one mark for each correct answer)

1 C **2** B **3** B **4** C **5** C **6** A **7** C **8** A

Part 2 (one mark for each correct answer)

9 (highly) stressful / (high) stress **10** logical
11 computer screen / computer
12 (an) identity parade(s) / (a) line(-)up(s) / (an) ID parade(s)
13 race / (skin) colour / colour (skin) / race and colour **14** (self)(-)confidence
15 long(-)term **16** source/origin **17** language

Part 3 (one mark for each correct answer)

18 C **19** B **20** A **21** A **22** B

Part 4 (one mark for each correct answer)

23 B **24** C **25** B **26** B **27** C **28** A

Transcript

Cambridge Certificate of Proficiency in English Listening Test. Test 2.

I'm going to give you the instructions for this test.

I'll introduce each part of the test and give you time to look at the questions.

At the start of each piece you'll hear this sound:

tone

You'll hear each piece twice.

Remember, while you're listening, write your answers on the question paper.

You'll have five minutes at the end of the test to copy your answers onto the separate answer sheet.

There will now be a pause. Please ask any questions now, because you must not speak during the test.

[pause]

PART 1

Now open your question paper and look at Part One.

[pause]

You'll hear four different extracts. For questions 1 to 8, choose the answer (A, B or C) which fits best according to what you hear. There are two questions for each extract.

Extract 1

[pause]

tone

Well, in the late twentieth century, tourists became the aristocrats of the new world order. They were pampered and protected wherever they went; they were treated with deference. The holiday companies tried to tailor the holiday experience to their clients' expectations, creating sort of safe havens for tourists, rather than tailoring their expectations to suit the country they were visiting – to what the host country could really provide. And so, when something happened which allowed them to get a glimpse of the real life of the country, they were unprepared and it tended to be an unpleasant experience; it pricked the bubble in which the tourist was travelling and they went back home even more convinced that everything foreign is dangerous.

It's a sad fact were you to have done a quick poll at any airport in western Europe, say, in the 1980s, and you had asked tourists what they knew of the country they'd just been to, you wouldn't have got very far.

[pause]

tone

[The recording is repeated.]

[pause]

Extract 2 [pause]

tone

In the sixteenth century, a huge and intricate map of London was created. The map-makers climbed various church towers – London was awash with churches at that time – and sketched out what they could see from the top of each one. If you like, it's a patchwork of triangles, with things omitted, buildings being moved round. For instance, you'll always see the handsome facade of the buildings. Obviously, if you'd been totally truthful, you'd have seen a lot of boring backyards. It's essentially a bird's-eye view of London, with the perspectives played around with, so while it appears that you're looking at a map, you're actually looking at a plan of the town with buildings cleverly juxtaposed on top of it.

Nobody seriously bought this map to get from A to B. What they really wanted was a view of a powerful city which they were associated with. And it's because of that, that whoever produced it was prepared to invest an awful lot to have it done, and anyone who acquired it had to pay a lot for the privilege.

[pause]

tone

[The recording is repeated.]

[pause]

Extract 3 [pause]

tone

Sue: Well, you must admit that thirties films about Egyptian mummies are regarded as ripe nonsense even by the standards of Hollywood horror films. I think it's amazing that they've brought out a new version. I wasn't convinced. What about you, Pete?

Pete: Well, I saw the original and the bare bones of the plot are very close to that, but in style it's different – they've gone for the action/adventure and comedy feel and they fall between all these stools, really.

Sue: Um, I found the characters one-dimensional and the gags when they're there, and they're there all the time, really don't work.

Pete: That's the main flaw with it. You have this thing now that the hero has to be a wise-cracking hero. I think this is very much a film made by design and committee where the good guy always has to have a line to deliver when something happens. As a result, all tension is undercut and any potential horror evaporates – you're just dulled.

[pause]

tone

[The recording is repeated.]

[pause]

Extract 4 [pause]

tone

Until recently, the operas of the eighteenth-century composer Handel were considered to be rather tedious, with tortuous plots and a static dramatic presentation. Yet there was almost a reverential attitude to them because it was felt that what you were doing by staging one was recreating the past through a kind of musical archaeology. Everything in these operas revolves around the rigid musical convention in which a singer stands on stage without moving and sings a long solo aria with built-in repetitions and embellishments designed to show her virtuosity. But one of the great discoveries we've made recently, through inventive stage directors and a new breed of singers, is that, for all the contrivance and formality of Handel's operas, there is an incredible resource of passion, and somehow it is stronger for the fact that it is presented to you, the audience, in a very controlled way. You feel these emotions . . . um . . . forcing the conventions, you know, testing them, pushing them to extremes. You feel the conventions are about to burst with the weight of this emotional outpouring. And it's one of the most exciting qualities in Handel's work.

[pause]

tone

[The recording is repeated.]

[pause]

That's the end of Part One.

Now turn to Part Two.

[pause]

PART 2

You will hear part of a radio programme about the difficulties faced by witnesses and by the police after a crime has been committed. For questions 9 to 17, complete the sentences with a word or short phrase.

You now have forty-five seconds in which to look at Part Two.

[pause]

tone

When a crime's been committed, the police often call on the general public for help. They need witnesses; they depend on the witness's eyes and ears to help track down the culprit. Acting as a witness calls for an accurate memory of events which have generally happened very quickly and under highly stressful circumstances. Not surprisingly, eye-witness memory has become a study for psychologists like myself.

I've been, first of all, evaluating the new systems used by the police to help witnesses reconstruct the face of the suspect. This new system has taken into account how we recognise facial features. The old system, photofit, where you had to piece together the eyes and then the mouth etc. of the suspect, was developed from a logical, rather than a psychological, analysis. It rather assumed people could look at isolated features and pick out an appropriate pair of eyes and so on. But in fact, people tend to remember faces as wholes, rather than a collection of features. So now we allow witnesses to work with a complete face on a computer screen and they can swap features in and out and make a much more accurate judgement about the degree of resemblance, in context. But what we don't know at the end of the day is whether witnesses are able to make more recognisable likenesses than they used to.

Another way for the police to ask for the help of witnesses is by using identity parades. This is where the police line up similar-looking people for the witnesses to identify the possible suspect. Unfortunately, one in five picks out someone who acts as a foil, someone known to be innocent.

One thing that has been researched over the last ten years is how the witness's race compared with the suspect's, how they match up – white people are better able to discriminate amongst other white people, for example. So this is something which is a major factor in trying to identify which witnesses are going to be the best at recalling these things. Another major factor which influences our accuracy is the amount of time which has passed since an event took place. And a lot of the indicators that people may think are good, like the confidence that a witness feels, is not actually as good a clue to their accuracy as we would hope. You often get these people saying, 'Yes, that's the one who did it. I'm positive of it.' But the person identified is not the suspect.

And another important question is, do older adults differ from younger ones in their memory for events? We know a lot about how older adults perform in conventional experiments where we might give them lists of words to remember or whatever. And we know that older adults are poorer at long-term memory than they are at short-term memory. We also know they tend to be poor at things like, did they read it or did they see it? Did Mr X tell them this fact or Mr Y? In other words that is, making decisions about the source of the memory.

So how have we gone about exploring these questions?

We show people a controlled event using videos depicting crimes and then after some delay we ask them a series of questions about the event. Unfortunately, it's too soon to be able to come to any firm conclusions.

And we've also done research which shows that the language an older adult uses is different from that of a younger adult. Most policemen are quite young, and many witnesses and victims of crime are quite old, and maybe the older adult's memory is not being fully used because of the communication problems.

So we're very much hoping that the results of our research make an impact on police procedure . . .

[pause]

Now you'll hear Part Two again.

tone

[The recording is repeated.]

[pause]

That's the end of Part Two.

Now turn to Part Three.

[pause]

PART 3

You will hear a radio interview with Diana Boardman, the manager of an orchestra. For questions 18 to 22, choose the answer (A, B, C or D) which fits best according to what you hear.

You now have one minute in which to look at Part Three.

[pause]

tone

Interviewer: I'm delighted to have with me today Diana Boardman, Manager of the Starlight Symphony Orchestra which is playing here in London at the moment. Diana, there are a lot of symphony orchestras, aren't there?

Diana: Yes, there are a number of orchestras around the country, but the Starlight Symphony Orchestra has its home in London and is traditionally an orchestra that plays contemporary music.

Interviewer: I notice on the programme that you play some of the popular classics like Tchaikovsky, but there's also a very high proportion of world premieres – new commissions like Tim Cartwright, Mark Westerman.

Diana: Yes, that's right. I think that's really what makes the orchestra exceptional amongst many orchestras. As I said, the orchestra has always had new writers very much at the heart – it's what the players are most skilled in and if you look back over the orchestra's history and the people it's been associated with, it's always been in that area of music.

Interviewer: We also know though that modern music is the least well attended in the concert programme . . .

Diana: Yes.

Interviewer: So is it a policy to sort of slip them in between better-known pieces . . . ?

Diana: That's the way we do it. I mean, I think there are only two ways you can programme contemporary music – you can either do that or you can go all out and programme an entire evening of contemporary music and make that an event in itself but there's a high risk to it.

Interviewer: Now there's a new piece by Julie Turnbull – one of the very few women composers represented.

Diana: That's right.

Interviewer: Do you think we're seeing a new trend for women artists?

Diana: It's certainly there . . . I mean I don't think you can single out classical music as a particular case – it's there across all the art forms in many different ways. I think it's a question of where we take things from here. We can't change what's happened in the past but it's a question of where we go from here.

Interviewer: It's an extraordinary fact, though, that there are more men in the audiences of classical music than there are women. Why do you suppose that is?

Diana: Certainly if you compare it to the ballet or the theatre worlds, that is the case. I think it's just because men have traditionally been more involved and so they're more attracted to it. I mean it's only in the last sort of five, ten years perhaps that if you go into an orchestral concert, you do see a good number of women on the stage.

Interviewer: I think that's particularly true of *your* orchestra. So, how did you come into arts administration?

Diana: Just by accident, really. I started working in Australia when I left university. I wanted to find a job that was interesting and challenging and I was lucky enough to be employed by the City of Sydney *Eisteddfod*, which is a three-week festival of competitions taken very seriously by the people that enter it, and at that time it wasn't necessarily a career in arts administration that I'd thought about. Most of my colleagues were trying to be merchant bankers or computer operators . . . erm, but I kept on with it and I've ended up where I am now.

Interviewer: Now you're going to be responsible for an educational initiative by the BBC, what's that?

[pause]

Now you'll hear Part Three again.

tone

[The recording is repeated.]

[pause]

That's the end of Part Three.

Now turn to Part Four.

[pause]

PART 4

You will hear Colin Beattie, the presenter of a radio arts programme, talking to Annie Watson, a critic, about a new TV drama series which stars an actor called Richard Garrard. For questions 23 to 28, decide whether the opinions are expressed by only one of the speakers, or whether the speakers agree. Write A for Annie, C for Colin, or B for both, where they agree.

You now have thirty seconds in which to look at Part Four.

[pause]

tone

Colin: With me today I have the critic Annie Watson, and we'll be discussing a new TV drama called *Man of Stone*. The lead character is played by the actor Richard Garrard, whose face is best known to us from television drama and film, usually in the menacing supporting role, which he does beautifully.

Annie: Mm . . . a role he has off to perfection, although this latest series does twist the typecasting slightly to have him as a loveable rogue.

Colin: A detective, called Jake incidentally, with a heart of gold . . . not particularly original. Episode one starts in action-packed London, but the camera soon focuses on Cardiff, which I thought set this series a little above the formulaic drama series about the eccentric professional with a complicated personal life.

Annie: Umm . . . I think the fact it's filmed there is very refreshing because there are so many series set in other UK cities.

Colin: Now, Annie, you've seen the first two episodes. The first ten minutes of the first episode is completely different from the rest, it's absolutely full of action, isn't it?

Annie: Well, I think that's a concession to the people who need an exciting bit to use for publicity purposes – and in this case it certainly seems to pay off.

Colin: It's that that makes you tune in to the first episode.

Annie: But it certainly calms down a bit in episode two, though. In fact, the first episode just sets the scene. It was unnecessary to explain in such boring detail the machinations of Garrard's character, Jake, not wanting to move but having to anyway.

Colin: But the way it established Jake's relationship with his daughter was very touching.

Annie: A bit on the sugary side, I thought. But with everyone else he seems to show nothing but contempt.

Colin: That's a little harsh, isn't it?

Annie: Maybe. But getting back to the series, you must agree it's really slow and perfunctory.

Colin: Come now, it's old-fashioned in that way and that's what I liked about it, because it's not, in the way that so many TV series are at the moment, cut very quickly with music thrown in. The camera lingers and there's great composition.

Annie: I don't really think it deserves such a eulogy but I'm sure it'll get . . .

[pause]

Now you'll hear Part Four again.

tone

[The recording is repeated.]

[pause]

That's the end of Part Four.

There will now be a pause of five minutes for you to copy your answers onto the separate answer sheet. Be sure to follow the numbering of all the questions.

Note: Stop/Pause the recording here and time five minutes. In the exam candidates will be reminded when there is **one** minute remaining.

[pause]

That's the end of the test. Please stop now. Your supervisor will now collect all the question papers and answer sheets.

Test 3 Key

Paper 1 Reading (1 hour 30 minutes)

Part 1 (one mark for each correct answer)

1 D 2 A 3 B 4 B 5 D 6 A 7 C 8 A 9 D
10 A 11 B 12 A 13 D 14 A 15 C 16 B 17 D
18 C

Part 2 (two marks for each correct answer)

19 B 20 D 21 C 22 B 23 A 24 D 25 D 26 C

Part 3 (two marks for each correct answer)

27 E 28 A 29 H 30 C 31 G 32 D 33 B

Part 4 (two marks for each correct answer)

34 B 35 C 36 D 37 A 38 A 39 C 40 B

Paper 2 Writing (2 hours)

Task-specific mark schemes

Question 1: Great Achievers

Content
Proposal must:
- name and justify choice of person
- describe aspects of person's life to be included
- explain how exhibition can reflect person's achievements

Range
Language for justifying, describing and/or narrating, suggesting and explaining.

Appropriacy of register and format
Register consistently appropriate for proposal for college members.
NB may be directed at college Principal **or** fellow students.

Organisation and cohesion
Clear organisation of ideas, possibly with headings.
Appropriate introduction and conclusion.

Target reader
Would understand why the person has been suggested and how his/her achievements could best be reflected in the exhibition.

Question 2: Wedding Celebrations

Content
Article must describe a typical wedding and explain why such weddings are so memorable. NB: explanation may well be covered in the description.

Range
Language of description, explanation – may also include evaluation.

Appropriacy of register and format
Register consistently appropriate for article in magazine.

Organisation and cohesion
Clear organisation and development of ideas.

Target reader
Would understand how weddings are celebrated, and writer's view of their special and memorable quality.

Question 3: Film Review

Content
Review must identify and describe a particular film and explain reasons for its continuing popularity.

Range
Language of description/narration, evaluation and explanation.

Appropriacy of register and format
Register consistently appropriate for general interest magazine.

Organisation and cohesion
Clearly organised, moving from description/narration to evaluation/explanation.

Target reader
Would have a clear impression of the film and understand writer's reason for thinking it will remain successful.

Question 4: Town Library

Content
Letter should attempt to explain under-use of library and suggest ways to attract readers by improvements/innovations.

Range
Language for explaining/hypothesising and suggesting.

Appropriacy of register and format
Register consistently appropriate for a letter to newspaper.

Organisation and cohesion
Appropriate opening and closing sentences – clear organisation of ideas.

Target reader
Would understand writer's explanation and suggestions.

Question 5(a): The Colour of Blood

Content
Description of two episodes which build suspense and maintain interest:
- the events in the agricultural college
- the ride in the police car
- the hospital meeting with Jan Ley
- the meeting with trade unionists
- the final scene in the cathedral

Explanation of how suspense is conveyed in these episodes.
(Underlined points must be included. Bulleted points are suggested examples.)

Range
Language of description, narration, explanation and evaluation.

Appropriacy of register and format
Register consistently appropriate for review in student magazine.

Organisation and cohesion
Clearly organised ideas.
Appropriate introduction and conclusion.

Target reader
Would understand what happened during these episodes, how the suspense was built up and interest maintained.

Question 5(b): The Go-Between

Content
Analysis of cricket match and description of aspects of it illustrating social divide:
- possible reference to other episodes in the novel illustrating social divide

Assessment of how far quotation is true.
(Underlined points must be included. Bulleted point may be included.)

Range
Language of description, narration, assessment.

Appropriacy of register and format
Register consistently appropriate for essay for tutor.

Organisation and cohesion
Clear organisation of ideas.
Appropriate conclusion.

Target reader
Would have a clear idea of the social background to the story and would understand the writer's assessment of it.

Question 5(c): Things Fall Apart

Content
Description of how life is governed by beliefs and customs of the clan:
social organisation within the village determines:
- family life – wives in separate huts
- differentiated tasks / farming for men and women

customs include:
- the week of peace – to ensure good harvest
- Feast of the New Yam
- betrothal ceremonies
- funeral rites

beliefs include:
- abhorrence of the unnatural – twins abandoned
- Okonkwo's father cannot be buried
- Okonkwo's body cannot be touched

ideas of justice:
- account for Okonkwo's exile
- Ikemefuna's presence in the village and his death

(Underlined points must be included. Bulleted points are suggested examples.)

Range
Language of description, narration, explanation and recommendation.

Appropriacy of register and format
Register consistently appropriate for report for reading group – headings would be acceptable.

Organisation and cohesion
Clear organisation of ideas.
Appropriate opening and conclusion.

Target reader
Would have a clear idea of some of the customs and beliefs of the clan, understand how these govern the lives of the people of Umuofia and be able to decide whether this was a suitable book for the reading group.

Paper 3 Use of English (1 hour 30 minutes)

Part 1 (one mark for each correct answer)

1 put **2** what **3** become **4** make **5** there
6 although/though/while/whilst **7** up **8** those **9** on **10** as
11 one **12** view **13** irrespective/regardless **14** such **15** a

Part 2 (one mark for each correct answer)

16 characteristic **17** recognisable/recognizable **18** unceremoniously
19 independent **20** extraordinary **21** rigidity **22** zealous
23 conservative **24** surrounding **25** increasingly

Part 3 (two marks for each correct answer)

26 fail **27** short **28** turn **29** account **30** blocked **31** deal

Part 4 (one mark for each correct answer)

32 Selena know/realise/suspect (1) + **how** difficult/hard it will be to (1)
33 **made** an immediate/instant (1) + impression on/upon (1)

34 put me (1) + at (my) **ease** with (1)
35 was no vegetation (1) + **whatsoever** (growing) in (1)
36 no circumstances (1) + will/shall we **ever** do business (1)
37 **came** to (1) + the conclusion (that) (1)
38 was in no **mood** / wasn't / was not in the/a/any **mood** (1) + for going out / to go out (1)
39 was taken **aback** (1) + by the news of the (1)
NB: the mark scheme for Part 4 may be expanded with other appropriate answers.

Part 5 (questions 40–43 two marks for each correct answer)

40 Modern cars are (so) quiet that the writer/he is aware of the noise (of the tyres) AND the noise of tyre rumble is more noticeable.
Both ideas required for the mark.
41 Explanation of the idea of 'subjectively' e.g. individuals respond differently to car noise. <u>Different from / contrasting with</u> explanation of scientific measurement e.g. whereas scientists will produce one objective result/measurement. Clear explanation of both parts of this contrast required.
42 Dismay (allow <u>In dismay</u>). No other additions other than a lead-in, e.g. The word is . . . . No alternatives.
43 Rousing. No additions other than a lead-in, e.g. The word is . . . . No alternatives.
44 Award up to four marks for content. The paragraph should include the following points:
- i (A majority of) drivers like noise evidence that car systems are working / in good order.
- ii (Most) drivers like engine noise AND/OR Car drivers like an engine noise which matches their expectations of the car.
- iii (Loud/fast) music can lead drivers to drive badly AND/OR Rousing rock music can make drivers aggressive.
- iv Loud music reduces the ability of drivers to think clearly.

Paper 4 Listening (40 minutes approximately)

Part 1 (one mark for each correct answer)

1 B **2** C **3** C **4** A **5** C **6** A **7** A **8** B

Part 2 (one mark for each correct answer)

9 artist(s) and writer(s) (in either order)
10 conservationists / the conservationist **11** (the) water(-)plants
12 energy/energies **13** m/March **14** agriculture/farming
15 (very) uneven **16** w/Wildlife t/Trust
17 p/Plan of a/Action (for the hare)

Part 3 (one mark for each correct answer)

18 D **19** C **20** C **21** C **22** B

Part 4 (one mark for each correct answer)

23 F **24** M **25** B **26** M **27** F **28** B

Transcript

Cambridge Certificate of Proficiency in English Listening Test. Test 3.

I'm going to give you the instructions for this test.

I'll introduce each part of the test and give you time to look at the questions.

At the start of each piece you'll hear this sound:

tone

You'll hear each piece twice.

Remember, while you're listening, write your answers on the question paper.

You'll have five minutes at the end of the test to copy your answers onto the separate answer sheet.

There will now be a pause. Please ask any questions now, because you must not speak during the test.

[pause]

PART 1

Now open your question paper and look at Part One.

[pause]

You'll hear four different extracts. For questions 1 to 8, choose the answer (A, B or C) which fits best according to what you hear. There are two questions for each extract.

Extract 1

[pause]

tone

Presenter: First on the programme today, we'll discuss the consultation document the UK airport authorities have just brought out, as part of their forward planning for the next thirty years. Of course, thirty years from now, we might be exploring the option of shuttle flights to Mars, but that's by-the-by. This document is concerned with more mundane, in fact, strictly down-to-earth considerations – delays, cancellations, lost baggage, congestion, the potential development of the air-freight sector, the integration of airports with the surface transportation infrastructure – hardly fly-me-to-the-moon stuff! But above all, its headline target is to give the travelling public a better deal. I asked the transport minister, Helen Fraser, to comment.

Helen: We have to strike a balance. The government certainly won't be committing itself to providing massive resources. Even if we can see the number of passengers is going to double, we can't necessarily double the number of runways, and the public will have to accept that. People are very keen to fly, but nobody's too keen to have a runway near them. So we have to talk about it thoroughly, and this document's a useful step in the consultative process.

[pause]

tone

[The recording is repeated.]

[pause]

Extract 2

[pause]

tone

My husband forgot my birthday this year, and he minded more than I did! I'm afraid that's what happens when you get to my age – birthdays lose their resonance and you're lucky if they're acknowledged at all. Some people would say you're luckier if they go unacknowledged, but I wouldn't go that far. But there again, it's more important that he remembers the kids' birthdays, isn't it? Be that as it may, in the event, he could see that I was a bit put out, because there is a residual excitement there, there's no getting away from it. It's nothing to do with getting older, although when I was nine or ten that was all-important . . . to think I used to long for the day when I'd be married with kids . . . No, what I feel now is more a little thrill, bred of nostalgia for the old excitement I used to feel, you know, about the attention, the presents and being more grown up; notching up another year towards adulthood.

[pause]

tone

[The recording is repeated.]

[pause]

Extract 3

[pause]

tone

Woman: Frankly I don't see why, just because a museum is for science and technology and not ancient artefacts and paintings, that means it's got to go down-market and have all these interactive exhibits, you know, pushing buttons and flashing lights.

Man: It stands to reason that they are pitched at a younger audience – school parties, kids with parents etc. and I'm afraid it's just no longer the case that kids will wander around in awe looking at a lot of old engine exhibits in glass boxes or drawers full of nuts and bolts. They won't put up with it, and if the numbers don't come in through the doors, then the museum is answerable – which is just what happened in Belton.

Woman: But that means, as usual, we're pandering to the lowest common denominator. Quoting examples of failed museums is not enough. More thorough investigation needs to be done. How do we know that customers won't like a few more traditional exhibits? I know my kids do and I don't think they're exceptional.

Man: That'll mean more money going into research, instead of into the museums themselves.

[pause]

tone

[The recording is repeated.]

[pause]

Extract 4

[pause]

tone

This is an extremely witty book, written in a racy style. It moves along at a great pace, the descriptions are crisp, the action dramatic. In fact, I've only got one reservation, but I fear it's an insurmountable one, because this is in fact an historical novel, dealing with the life and experiences of Mary Queen of Scots – so we're going back four centuries. And apart from inventing dialogue between people who were not actually contemporaries, the writer has peppered the story with anachronisms so gross as to be almost a source of entertainment in themselves. I found myself half expecting a bicycle or train to appear amongst the carts and carriages at any moment. And I wish I could believe that she was writing a spoof, but sadly this is not the case. And this is the aspect of the book which will spoil it for the intelligent reader. Although, if you can suspend disbelief for a bit, in favour of an evening of pure escapism, it's actually a jolly good read, for all its shortcomings.

[pause]

tone

[The recording is repeated.]

[pause]

That's the end of Part One.

Now turn to Part Two.

[pause]

PART 2

You will hear part of a radio talk about a small mammal called the brown hare. For questions 9 to 17, complete the sentences with a word or short phrase.

You now have forty-five seconds in which to look at Part Two.

[pause]

tone

The long-legged, long-eared brown hare, which looks like a taller cousin of the common rabbit, is an enigmatic creature. Shrouded in mystery and steeped in folklore, it attracts a wide range of admirers. To writers and artists, it's an endless source of inspiration; to hunters it's a challenging game animal as it dashes for cover across the winter fields. And, more practically, to some farmers it's an annoying pest. And although it's still familiar on farmland in many parts of Britain, conservationists are starting to detect a worrying problem because in recent years the brown hare hasn't been thriving and the population is in decline.

What's more, this doesn't seem to be particularly connected with habitat. Hares are often to be found beside ditches where water plants provide plenty of cover during the day. At night, because they like to be where they can see danger coming, they make their way to open ground. Their main predators are foxes, but adult hares can easily outrun them. If a fox comes into a field where hares are, they won't pay much attention to it until it gets within about fifty metres. At that point, the hare stands on its hind legs and looks directly at the fox. This is actually a signal which says to the fox, 'I've seen you so there's no point in chasing me.' It's a behaviour known as 'pursuit deterrence', and it's one that's beneficial to both animals because they don't waste the energy which would be expended in a fruitless chase.

The fox and the hare often turn up in folklore, where hares are often associated with madness. This may stem from the fact that hares are basically nocturnal animals. People used to look out over open fields on clear moonlit nights and see hares behaving strangely. In the breeding season, which lasts from January to July, they may be seen chasing each other across fields and engaging in what look like boxing matches. In Britain at least, hares are traditionally thought to 'go mad' in March, but this is simply the time of the year when they're most evident to the casual observer. The nights are getting shorter, so they're forced out more during the hours of daylight, whilst the crops in the fields have not yet grown to a height where they conceal the hare's activities.

So what is happening to this familiar creature? Some surveys, carried out in the 1990s, tried to determine trends in the hare population. In recent years, there've been many changes in agriculture that should have benefited hares. Fields have become larger, for example, whilst field crops have often replaced livestock farming. Both trends produce just the sort of habitat which hares seek out. But the population was in fact found to have declined by around ten per cent over five years. Thanks to the surveys, there now exists a clear picture of the national distribution of hares and it's very uneven. Hare numbers have long been susceptible to annual fluctuation but, even taking this into account, a pattern emerges; a few isolated pockets with reasonable numbers of animals are interspersed with quite large areas with very few or none at all.

In response to these findings, a number of schemes are being established and run by the Wildlife Trust. These are designed to show that game animals, wildlife and farming can co-exist quite happily. In the areas covered by the schemes, vegetation is allowed to grow high in certain places with more banks and ditches designed to provide protection for hares. With careful and judicious management, it should be possible to increase hare numbers quite dramatically and quickly within a limited area. The long-term conservation goal, however, is to achieve reasonable numbers of hares across the whole country. A Plan of Action for the hare was published in 1995. It has a highly ambitious target for the hare's recovery to ensure that the population recoups its decline by 2010. Thus we hope that in the future . . .

[pause]

Now you'll hear Part Two again.

tone

[The recording is repeated.]

[pause]

That's the end of Part Two.

Now turn to Part Three.

[pause]

PART 3

You will hear an interview with a British film director, Ann Howard, who has recently made a film in Hollywood. For questions 18 to 22, choose the answer (A, B, C or D) which fits best according to what you hear.

You now have one minute in which to look at Part Three.

[pause]

tone

Interviewer: With us today in the studio is the film director, Ann Howard. Ann, your early success gave you the opportunity to travel to the USA to work in Hollywood. Would you say you have a good relationship with the American film business?

Ann Howard: Oh, everybody has a tough relationship with the American film industry, you know. Hollywood's got this ability to love the success of the films you've done independently and then want to destroy that very fact, really; to buy you and then to make you into something very different.

Interviewer: Their studio system did little for the one film you made over there, did it?

Ann Howard: Yeah, it was a bit messed up. I had a bit of trouble there.

Interviewer: It's a shame because you can see the original concept has an awful lot going for it.

Ann Howard: Yeah, but I shouldn't really be allowed to make a comedy. It's not in my temperament, really! I can't even tell a joke! So there were a lot of factors at work in all that.

Interviewer: There were several script writers involved, weren't there?

Ann Howard: Yes, quite a few. I mean, I wrote the script and there were American characters in it, so when I showed it to the studio, they said, 'Well, let's define these American characters more clearly. Let's build up the American sequences' and all that kind of thing. 'So let's work with this writer and that writer' and in the end there were three or four of us working on it and it got a bit confusing.

Interviewer: And the ship sort of sails away at that point, doesn't it?

Ann Howard: Right, it does. Yeah. But you've still got to direct the film, you know. And you've got to deal with everything. And it was quite an interesting experience. I still got a lot out of directing it, you know. And then we cut the movie together and I went through the experience of previews, which I hadn't been through before.

Interviewer: Now, this is where they put it to test audiences, don't they?

Ann Howard: Yeah, they do it very scientifically, actually. And the answers are always the same. It's amazing. You preview it in Los Angeles and they say, 'Let's try New York to see if we get different responses', then they're exactly the same in New York as in Los Angeles.

Interviewer: But surely that audience knows they're watching it under very strange circumstances?

Ann Howard: Yeah, too right, you've got a bunch of self-appointed critics because generally you don't look at a film and fill out a card. First of all, you should choose to see a movie. When you pay for the ticket, you've accepted some level of involvement with the film.

Interviewer: It's like a contract, isn't it?

Ann Howard: Yeah, but when you go to a test audience showing, you haven't done that. You're going to be a kind of privileged person.

Interviewer: And these people can cause changes to occur?

Ann Howard: Well, yeah. They can do. They have approval ratings. Then they have to say if they will recommend it to their friends. And so you have to get definitely or probably on that, combined with excellent or very good on 75–80% of the cards, and if not they put you back in the mincer and grind you up ready to spit you out again.

Interviewer: It makes you wonder what would have happened to the great classics if they'd had to go through that, doesn't it?

Ann Howard: Well, they always did it, even Chaplin used to preview his films, you know. I mean, it's a useful tool as long as it's in the hands of the film maker. If you direct a movie, you want to know about points that maybe don't reach an audience and you realise that very quickly if you show it to two or three hundred people.

Interviewer: But then you're still relying on your own judgement ultimately, aren't you?

Ann Howard: Yeah. It's when it's used as a marketing tool or as a tool to make the films accessible to the blandest, most middle-of-the-road audience that you get problems.

Interviewer: Yeah. You get movies that all look like American television.

Ann Howard: Yeah, they all look the same, don't they? It's America, when you go there . . .

[pause]

Now you'll hear Part Three again.

tone

[The recording is repeated.]

[pause]

That's the end of Part Three.

Now turn to Part Four.

[pause]

PART 4

You will hear part of a radio discussion in which two friends, Frieda and Martin, are being interviewed about tidiness. For questions 23 to 28, decide whether the opinions are expressed by only one of the speakers, or whether the speakers agree. Write F for Frieda, M for Martin, or B for both, where they agree.

You now have thirty seconds in which to look at Part Four.

[pause]

tone

Interviewer: This week in our series 'Obsessions' we're going to talk about tidiness. With me are Frieda Keele and Martin Robinson. Frieda, why do you think that some of us have full control over our possessions and are disciplined about what we have and where we keep everything, while others live in a constant muddle of things we can't bear to put away, let alone throw away?

Frieda: For me tidiness is something I've always been used to. I've never even thought about it. My mother was incredibly houseproud and I guess I just learnt it from her. If your parents lived in a muddle then I suppose you will too.

Martin: My parents didn't live in a mess, but my room was my own. Thank goodness, my mother just accepted there were certain things I just had to have. They were part of me. Didn't you have your treasures, Frieda?

Frieda: Oh, yes, there were five-minute wonders, but they were always tidy, and every so often I'd throw some out when they weren't useful any more.

Martin: Oh no. I treasured things for ten or fifteen years.

Frieda: So they served some purpose, did they?

Martin: Oh no, I never used them, I just kept them in my bedroom all that time, a bit like a squirrel, you know . . .

Frieda: But what happened to them, where are they now, these things that were such an important part of your life?

Martin: I bet if I looked, they'd all be in a box somewhere in the attic in my mum's house.

Frieda: My mother would've thrown them out, because she chucked everything out, everything that wasn't useful to her . . . I thought all mothers do this, you know . . . in the bin!

Martin: That must have been a nightmare! No, my mum just . . . let me muddle along. Occasionally she'd say, 'Martin, I want to clean your room tomorrow, so will you clear it a bit?' She was great like that. Never any hassle. That's why I'm such a laid-back person, I think.

Frieda: And maybe why I'm so stressed.

Martin: Don't you think that tidiness is not a constant, it's in the eye of the beholder?

Frieda: I don't quite see what you mean, sorry?

Martin: I mean the room I work in at home now, it's appallingly untidy. There are layers of . . . paper and everything all over the floor. But that's the way I like to work.

Frieda: Now, that amazes me because I would have assumed that you were . . . the kind of . . . person like myself . . . I've an office where . . . I work from home . . . and I simply can't get down to work unless . . . everything is exactly where it ought to be. The desk has to be clear and . . .

Martin: Oh look, you've even done a sort of diagram of how you're going to organise the day . . . that gives me the shivers. It's so orderly!

Frieda: But I have to be orderly.

Martin: But I find that if I start tidying up, then I don't do any work at all because . . . tidying up is infinite . . . there's no end to it.

Frieda: But that's not so. Anyway, it's fantastic that feeling, when you've got . . . everything straight.

Martin: . . . And then you feel you've done a day's work, and so you don't do anything . . . constructive. Tidying is endlessly preparing the ground for some great work . . . but you risk never doing the great work! It's an illusion the tidying, just get on . . . with the job in hand, I say.

Frieda: Oh no, I couldn't . . . because for me it's not a displacement activity . . .

Martin: A what?

Frieda: You know, I'm not putting off anything by tidying up, it's just part of . . . routine . . . and here I am look . . . I'm called the scruffy one.

Martin: Wearing old jeans.

Frieda: And there's you in a collar and tie and everything . . . and yet you've got the untidy room.

Martin: Just goes to show, doesn't it?

Frieda: Umm.

Interviewer: And that's where we have to leave it today. Frieda, Martin, thank you.

[pause]

Now you'll hear Part Four again.

tone

[The recording is repeated.]

[pause]

That's the end of Part Four.

There will now be a pause of five minutes for you to copy your answers onto the separate answer sheet. Be sure to follow the numbering of all the questions.

Note: Stop/Pause the recording here and time five minutes. In the exam candidates will be reminded when there is **one** minute remaining.

[pause]

That's the end of the test. Please stop now. Your supervisor will now collect all the question papers and answer sheets.

Test 4 Key

Paper 1 Reading (1 hour 30 minutes)

Part 1 (one mark for each correct answer)

1 C 2 B 3 A 4 B 5 D 6 C 7 C 8 B 9 A
10 D 11 B 12 C 13 A 14 D 15 B 16 C 17 D
18 C

Part 2 (two marks for each correct answer)

19 B 20 A 21 D 22 B 23 D 24 C 25 A 26 C

Part 3 (two marks for each correct answer)

27 C 28 G 29 B 30 E 31 H 32 A 33 F

Part 4 (two marks for each correct answer)

34 B 35 B 36 D 37 B 38 A 39 C 40 D

Paper 2 Writing (2 hours)

Task-specific mark schemes

Question 1: Environment

Content
Article should discuss whether environmental crisis exists and how serious it is.

Major points for discussion:
- that our way of life is damaging the environment
- that natural resources are disappearing
- the possibility that lifestyle and attitudes can be changed

Range
Language for explaining, presenting/developing an argument, evaluating – may include hypothesising.

Appropriacy of register and format
Register consistently appropriate for magazine article.

Organisation and cohesion
Clear development of argument.
Appropriate introduction and conclusion.

Target reader
Would understand writer's views on the seriousness or otherwise of the environmental crisis.

Question 2: Personal Possessions

Content
Letter should describe the object and explain why the writer wants to keep it forever.

Range
Language of description and explanation.

Appropriacy of register and format
Register consistently appropriate for letter to magazine.

Organisation and cohesion
Clearly organised.
Suitable opening and concluding sentences.

Target reader
Would know what the object is like and understand its significance for the writer.

Question 3: Old Building

Content
Proposal should suggest two uses for the building and explain how these will improve life for young people.

Range
Language of recommendation, explanation and description.

Appropriacy of register and format
Register consistently appropriate for a proposal to the council.

Organisation and cohesion
Clear organisation, possibly with headings.

Target reader
Would understand the suggestions put forward and the benefits they would offer to young people.

Question 4: It All Worked Out Well

Content
Article should describe a difficult situation and explain how it resulted in a positive experience.

Range
Language of description, narration, explanation and evaluation.

Appropriacy of register and format
Register consistently appropriate for magazine article.

Organisation and cohesion
Early reference to reason for writing.
Clearly organised, moving from narration to explanation and suitable conclusion.

Target reader
Would understand the writer's experience, how the situation developed and its significance.

Question 5(a): The Colour of Blood

Content
Description of how Bem behaves in three locations and what this reveals about his character.
Suggested locations:
- agricultural college
- fields/countryside outside college
- church (flower arranger)
- railway station
- in the police car
- outside the church (leaflet distribution)
- in the hospital with Jan Ley
- in Jop's house
- in Mallinek Palace (PM's quarters)
- final scene in Cathedral

(Underlined points must be included. Bulleted points are suggested examples.)

Range
Language of description, narration and explanation.

Appropriacy of register and format
Register consistently appropriate for essay for tutor.

Organisation and cohesion
Clear development of ideas, description leading to explanation and appropriate conclusion.

Target reader
Would understand how Bem behaved and how his character was revealed in three episodes/locations.

Question 5(b): The Go-Between

Content
Explanation of how Leo relates to adults:
- fits into role as child in the household
- total confusion in the situation involving Marian and Ted

Description of adult world and values:
- organisation of the household
- picnics, tennis and swimming parties
- Lord T's values and beliefs
- Marian – selfish disregard for Leo's feelings
- Ted – honest, practical, bleak outlook on life

(Underlined points must be included. Bulleted points are suggested examples.)

Range
Language of description, narration and analysis.

Appropriacy of register and format
Register consistently appropriate for review in a local newspaper.

Organisation and cohesion
Clear organisation of ideas.

Target reader
Would understand Leo's relationship with adults at Brandham Hall.

Question 5(c): Things Fall Apart

Content
<u>Description of different cultures represented by Okonkwo and his people and the missionaries and colonial governors:</u>
People of Umuofia
- beliefs
- customs
- code of behaviour

Missionaries and governors
- establish trading post
- bring education
- bring new religion which appeals e.g. to Nwoye
- establish new laws and courts

<u>Assessment of extent to which the two learn to understand each other:</u>
- Okonkwo refuses to change, or try to understand
- others, e.g. Obierika, say there is no point in resisting
- some, like Nwoye, are converted and see good in what the missionaries are doing
- attitude of the Commissioner – an anthropological study
- understanding attitude of some missionaries (Mr Brown)
- intolerance of others (Mr Smith)
- villagers taken prisoner when they expected to have discussions
- court officials beat and insult prisoners

(Underlined points must be included. Bulleted points are suggested examples.)

Range
Language of description, narration and assessment.

Appropriacy of register and format
Register consistently appropriate for report for librarian – may have headings.

Organisation and cohesion
Clear organisation of ideas.
Description leading to assessment.

Target reader
Would understand something of the two cultures, would be able to assess the extent to which the people learn to understand each other and be able to decide if this was a suitable book for the exhibition.

Paper 3 Use of English (1 hour 30 minutes)

Part 1 (one mark for each correct answer)

1 a **2** in **3** each **4** its **5** what **6** their **7** how
8 however/nevertheless **9** less **10** so **11** like **12** next
13 carry **14** to **15** into

Part 2 (one mark for each correct answer)

16 accessible (NOT accessed) **17** leisurely **18** unforgettable
19 breath(-)taking **20** mountaineer(s) **21** erosion **22** challenging
23 imperceptibly **24** diversity/biodiversity (NOT diversification)
25 splendour/splendor

Part 3 (two marks for each correct answer)

26 report **27** board **28** natural **29** appearance **30** set
31 hot

Part 4 (one mark for each correct answer)

32 **it** not (1) + been for (1)
33 did with her money (1) + was no **concern** (1)
34 was on the **point** (1) + of leaving (the office) (1)
35 **sooner** had I got (1) + in(to) my car than (1)
36 took (absolutely) no (1) + **notice** (what(so)ever) of (1)
37 not the first **time** (1) + (that) Sally has run (1)
38 **better** known (1) + as a writer (of books) (1)
39 has been **brought** (1) + to my attention (1)
NB: the mark scheme for Part 4 may be expanded with other appropriate answers.

Part 5 (questions 40–43 two marks for each correct answer)

40 It shows the fact that brands are all around us / they dominate our lives OR it echoes the word landscape, NOT answers like 'There are so many brands in today's markets.'
41 (The verb is) decode. No further additions from the text unless 'decode' is highlighted.
42 Their work (in a call centre) / handling/dealing with (confused, demanding, anxious) customers NOT answers which refer to patience only
43 In the past the focus was on the relationship between the producer and the customer whereas now importance is placed on promoting the brand to employees. BOTH past and present reference essential.
44 Award up to four marks for content. The paragraph should include the following points:
- i Brands generate trust / sense of security / represent certainty / consistency of quality.
- ii Brands provide us with criteria / a set of values / a way by which we judge others.

iii Producers want to appear morally and socially responsible / people to ignore how goods are produced / people to identify with their philosophy.
iv Brands motivate employees to work hard / inspire employees with affection and loyalty.

Paper 4 Listening (40 minutes approximately)

Part 1 (one mark for each correct answer)

1 C 2 A 3 A 4 C 5 B 6 C 7 B 8 A

Part 2 (one mark for each correct answer)

9 feathers / (striking) plumage
10 (very) yellow-green / yellow (and) green (in either order but NOT yellow or green) **11** surface **12** diet/food/feeding **13** nesting
14 adult (population of) **15** soft(er) / a soft(er) call
16 (body) warmth/heat (NOT vigilance)
17 ill(-)health / poor health / bad health

Part 3 (one mark for each correct answer)

18 D **19** B **20** B **21** A **22** D

Part 4 (one mark for each correct answer)

23 B **24** W **25** S **26** S **27** B **28** B

Transcript

Cambridge Certificate of Proficiency in English Listening Test. Test 4.

I'm going to give you the instructions for this test.

I'll introduce each part of the test and give you time to look at the questions.

At the start of each piece you'll hear this sound:

tone

You'll hear each piece twice.

Remember, while you're listening, write your answers on the question paper.

You'll have five minutes at the end of the test to copy your answers onto the separate answer sheet.

There will now be a pause. Please ask any questions now, because you must not speak during the test.

[pause]

PART 1

Now open your question paper and look at Part One.

[pause]

You'll hear four different extracts. For questions 1 to 8, choose the answer (A, B or C) which fits best according to what you hear. There are two questions for each extract.

Extract 1 [pause]

tone

Interviewer: Do you think it's true that science fiction writing is still seen as being outside the literary mainstream?

Jim: Yes, and I think that's because literary critics on the whole are educated to think of literature as being – um – an interplay between characters, and science fiction isn't like that! It concerns humans struggling against something unknown, something that has to be grasped. And then personally what attracted me to it when I came back after an extended period travelling right away from ordinary society was that I saw it as the literature of outsiders.

Interviewer: At the start of the new millennium, so many people have said that all the predictions in science fiction films of the last fifty years were all completely wrong. Do you think they were?

Jim: I'm not sure that it's about prediction. For some writers it may be but – er – for me it's a kind of mythology. To take an example, the idea of a machine that's programmed to think of itself as human is in itself touching, even tragic.

Interviewer: A bit like something out of classical myth as well?

Jim: It is, yes.

[pause]

tone

[The recording is repeated.]

[pause]

Extract 2 [pause]

tone

The domestic cat has been part of everyday life in Europe for many hundreds of years. In fact, the first signs of a domestic cat in Britain come from an archaeological site dating from the Iron Age, the period that lasted from about 500 B.C. to the time of the Roman invasion in 55 B.C.

Another interesting thing is whether domestic cats were deliberately acquired the way farm animals were, or whether they just came along of their own accord and were tolerated by humans. I suspect the latter, in which case we could find their remains from a much earlier period.

The search for evidence to pin down the exact date of the domestic cat's arrival in Britain is made no easier by the fact that our own native wild cats, which were fairly widespread across the country, were likely to interbreed with domestic cats that had left their homes and become strays. As a result, one of the problems we always have is deciding whether a particular isolated bone is of a domestic cat or a local wild cat – there's very little difference between them.

[pause]

tone

[The recording is repeated.]

[pause]

Extract 3 [pause]

tone

Presenter: So what's the state of photojournalism today, Ian?

Ian: Well, in my view there are some remarkably high-calibre people out there and some promising young ones learning the ropes, but in many cases it will have to be a labour of love, since markets for exciting independent work are much thinner on the ground and that seems to be a well-established trend, and not just a temporary 'blip'.

Presenter: So why is it so problematic? There presumably was a time when photojournalists could more or less pick the publication where they 'placed' their work?

Ian: I think there's the globalisation of the market and there's been a shift in editorial attitudes.

Presenter: Why, what's changed?

Ian: Well, I think one of the aspects is it's very hard to find a story now that hasn't been covered to death already. Wherever there's news or worthwhile pictures you're going to find four or five different types of media trying to get to it. And the public have access to everything and their attention span's very short, so editors daren't print an in-depth analysis with a series of well-chosen images even two days after a world event.

[pause]

tone

[The recording is repeated.]

[pause]

Extract 4

[pause]

tone

With a new concert hall, you start with a basic shape that must accommodate anything from a guitar solo to a full 80-piece orchestra. To get that flexibility, you have to be able to change the acoustic conditions accordingly. We use several different methods to achieve this, such as soft panels that slide in and out of the room from slots in the ceiling; or maybe very large sound deflectors hanging above the stage; and you can actually increase or decrease the effective size of the room itself by putting in a series of gates or valves in the side walls which can be opened or closed. All this can make a real difference to the acoustics of the hall, but at a high cost.

When re-thinking an old concert hall, there are a lot of very low cost and relatively simple things that can be done to improve the sound quality when the basic shape cannot be altered. You can always simply move the aisle carpet or change the seats. And sometimes stripping off the layers of thin wood and old plaster to reveal the solid wall behind also helps, producing a significant improvement in orchestral sound quality.

[pause]

tone

[The recording is repeated.]

[pause]

That's the end of Part One.

Now turn to Part Two.

[pause]

PART 2

You will hear part of a radio programme about wildlife in which a researcher, Kevin Nelson, talks about a type of duck called the mallard, which he has been studying. For questions 9 to 17, complete the sentences with a word or short phrase.

You now have forty-five seconds in which to look at Part Two.

[pause]

tone

Interviewer: Ducks are present in just about every country in the world and are widely recognised as a result. Researcher Kevin Nelson has been looking at one type of duck in particular, the mallard. And he has made some very interesting discoveries. On a recent visit to London, he told us about them.

Kevin: It came as a bombshell to me. I'd spent years banging my head against a brick wall trying to figure out just what it was about the male mallard duck that the female found attractive. When I started out, I imagined it must be some aspect of the feathers because the male has very striking plumage, in contrast to the female. But this proved not to be the case. So I started looking at other things, such as size, behaviour, etc. But what became clear was that the thing females were actually paying attention to was the coloration of the male duck's mouthparts, what's known as the bill.

I realised that the more attractive males have flawless bills, very yellow-green, no blemishes, whilst others have more grey-green bills, often with little black spots on. And the bill is very important. The mallard uses it as a filter because this is not a diving duck, it doesn't catch fish or find things on the bottom of the rivers and lakes where it lives, it rather dabbles on the surface, the bill filtering out the plant and animal matter it depends on. And the key to all this is that the coloration of the bill can change on a much shorter time-scale than the feathers. The feathers that the duck grows in the autumn will stay with it through to the following June, but as the duck's diet changes, so does the colour of its bill. So by keeping an eye on that, the female can spot the best fed duck to be the father of her ducklings.

So I then asked myself, 'In that case, why is it that the male and female ducks have such different colouring?' And it seems actually that it's the female's brown inconspicuous plumage that is easier to explain. And that explanation lies in the fact that the female is particularly vulnerable to predators when she's nesting. The nest, which is often built up a waterside tree, is constructed using a combination of leaves and grass, and the female stays there for up to twenty-three days, during which time she is very vulnerable, despite the camouflage. So much so, actually, that an imbalance in the population results. At hatching, there's an equal number of male and female chicks, but in the adult population you often see what's called 'a pair and a spare', three ducks which go around together and the spare is often an extra male.

This also goes some way to explaining the male duck's relative silence. It's the female who makes the characteristic quacking sound as she keeps in touch with her chicks and warns of danger. The male has a softer call, rarely heard unless he is excited or alarmed.

The ducklings themselves are fairly independent, however, and can swim and feed themselves twelve hours after hatching. But within the first week or so of life, they lack the ability to generate their own body heat and so rely on the female duck for warmth. That's why you'll often see the ducklings clustered around the mother, and she can keep up to about fifteen with her in that way. One thing that interested me though, was the fact that you often see very large numbers of ducklings under the protection of one female. And this is because there's an interesting, and not uncommon, phenomenon amongst mallards. What happens is offspring are often abandoned by mothers who are in ill-health and these mothers may actually be making a wise decision. Because other mothers, better able to provide protection from predators, are quite happy to adopt ducklings which are not their own. You see, in this species, the mother can do this at very little extra cost, as these ducklings can feed themselves. After that initial first week, the female only has to provide vigilance for the whole group, regardless of its size. I once saw a mother with a group of sixty ducklings – it's a wonderful sight.

Interviewer: Kevin Nelson there, talking about the mallard duck.

[pause]

Now you'll hear Part Two again.

tone

[The recording is repeated.]

[pause]

That's the end of Part Two.

Now turn to Part Three.

[pause]

PART 3

You will hear an interview with Roland Brundy, the new chairman of the television channel GTV. For questions 18 to 22, choose the answer (A, B, C or D) which fits best according to what you hear.

You now have one minute in which to look at Part Three.

[pause]

tone

Heather: The appointment of Roland Brundy as chairman of GTV has been widely welcomed. I spoke to him earlier this week. Roland, ten years is a relatively long time in the life of a television channel. What trends do you think are going to have an impact on GTV during your reign as chairman?

Brundy: Well I think one of the most obvious is technology – the advent of digital radio and television and of course the increase in the number of channels in Britain. And all that is closely linked to competition; more channels means more choice for the consumer.

Heather: Whom do you regard as the competition?

Brundy: Everybody. The other channels, independent radio companies, satellite. It's by no means all bad, it forces GTV to sharpen up its act and with all the extra activity, it increases the pool of talent and ideas available, so competition isn't, er, a one-way street if you like.

Heather: So how do you think the competition should be tackled? Is it a case of trying to do the same thing except more or better or should you compete by offering something different – or should you do both?

Brundy: I don't think you can cover all angles. I think either you say you're going to take the competition head on and here's where we're going to find the resources to do it, this is where we're going to match the exponentially rising costs of sporting events, say, and films. Or you say we're not going to take them head on; we don't have the resources to do it, so we'll do something different.

Heather: You've mentioned sport and films – is that because they're areas where you're losing viewers to other channels or . . .

Brundy: Acquiring sporting events and movies is actually easy. You just write a bigger cheque than anyone else's. But it's not so easy to have the sort of standing you want in the arts – in drama – even if it's mainstream stuff, er, or something like current affairs. They require creativity, a corpus of people, a history – it all takes time, you can't just buy it.

Heather: So, how you react to competition can be a difficult decision to make.

Brundy: It can put you in a very invidious position. On the one hand, of course, you can do nothing and then people turn around and say look at fuddy duddy old GTV, they haven't even noticed what's going on in the market – they haven't changed anything. But if you do change or adapt you can get accused of copying – but who's copying whom?

Heather: Do you have a world view on technological change?

Brundy: A world view? Beware of broadcasters with world views! No, no I don't. I think you have to take note of what's happening – all the time – but restrain any fears you may have that it's all going to happen tomorrow as we're led to believe. I'm dubious about the pace of technological change and the way it affects broadcasters and viewers and I've learnt through the experience of the last ten years that technology doesn't drive this industry – in the end it serves it.

Heather: What do you think the main differences are between running a television channel and running any other type of business?

Brundy: Well, the first that springs to mind always is how you gauge your achievement. It's much less precise in this field – not less important but much harder to quantify. GTV has actually done some quite sensible things in trying to ascertain such things but where that hasn't been possible it's tried to identify the objectives it's aiming to achieve. I think the other difference is that GTV is a more important place than anywhere I've worked. It touches every aspect of life in this country. I mean without being too pompous, it's far more significant than the printing business, or a weekend commercial television company.

[pause]

Now you'll hear Part Three again.

tone

[The recording is repeated.]

[pause]

That's the end of Part Three.

Now turn to Part Four.

[pause]

PART 4

You will hear part of a radio discussion in which two actors, William and Sonia, talk about their profession. For questions 23 to 28, decide whether the opinions are expressed by only one of the speakers, or whether the speakers agree. Write W for William, S for Sonia, or B for both, where they agree.

You now have thirty seconds in which to look at Part Four.

[pause]

tone

Presenter: Welcome to 'Artscene'. With me today are the stage and film actors Sonia Neville and William Brady. I'd like to begin by asking you both what you do before rehearsals start. Do you read the whole script, or look just at your lines within the script, or focus on the main speeches within your lines, or what? Sonia?

Sonia: Well, some directors want you to know your lines by the time you get to the rehearsal stage.

William: Well, it is important to have read the script carefully, but I always work on the person before the words . . .

Sonia: Uh-huh, the character, the source of the speeches . . .

William: So I do extensive research and compare myself to the character. I see what I have that fits him and what I don't have. I find it quite a hard process and . . .

Sonia: Oh, I think one of the most important things about preparation for a part is to relax . . .

William: Lucky you! But you're not going to be acting by yourself – you're playing with somebody – so you can never know what you might have to respond to . . .

Sonia: But that's exactly what creates quality performances – if you all get it right!

Presenter: And, once you've arrived at a way of playing a character, do you stick with that or do you keep changing it as you keep performing the role? William?

William: Mmm . . . I find so much depends on the audience, the energy you get out there can vary. But, well . . .

Sonia: Ah, once I've arrived at my performance, I pretty well hold to it. OK, it can happen that someone reads a line with a different inflection or emphasis and then I find myself changing my reading because he's changed his. But then later I tend to decide, no, that's not it, I'd better keep it the way it was.

William: Now, of course, we both have experience of the stage and of film. I find the level of satisfaction is the same on camera. Don't you, Sonia?
Sonia: I suppose it is, but there are very different satisfactions. In the theatre, I enjoy the physicality of acting.
William: The overall discipline . . . you need more strength, more energy . . .
Sonia: I'm proud of the fact that I have that energy. In the theatre, the pleasures are immediate – you know exactly how you're doing it when you're doing it. And it's you who decides, really, how that is each time the curtain goes up.
William: It's your movements every time. Mind you, I've really had very good outings in film, so there's no reason for me to complain about the way it works.
Presenter: So what does a film assignment give a theatre actor, William?
William: I think it's learning the intricacies of letting the small things stand for themselves. In other words, having the confidence to do something on a small level and let it be seen by the camera . . .
Sonia: You can get away with things in the theatre that you can't in films. You can cover up certain deficiencies with a kind of theatricality, you can hide certain faults . . .
William: You can't do that in film because the camera picks up everything!
Presenter: I'd like to know what makes a good director from an actor's point of view. Sonia?
Sonia: I suppose it's a combination of things, really. I do like someone who is. . .

[pause]

Now you'll hear Part Four again.

tone

[The recording is repeated.]

[pause]

That's the end of Part Four.

There will now be a pause of five minutes for you to copy your answers onto the separate answer sheet. Be sure to follow the numbering of all the questions.

Note: Stop/Pause the recording here and time five minutes. In the exam candidates will be reminded when there is **one** minute remaining.

[pause]

That's the end of the test. Please stop now. Your supervisor will now collect all the question papers and answer sheets.

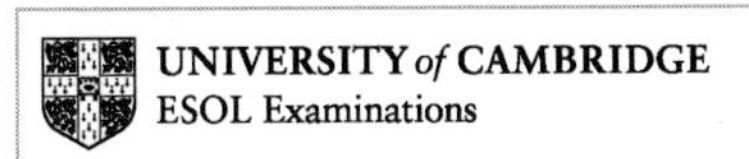

S A M P L E

Candidate Name
If not already printed, write name in CAPITALS and complete the Candidate No. grid (in pencil).

Candidate Signature

Examination Title

Centre

Supervisor:
If the candidate is ABSENT or has WITHDRAWN shade here

Centre No.

Candidate No.

Examination Details

0	0	0	0
1	1	1	1
2	2	2	2
3	3	3	3
4	4	4	4
5	5	5	5
6	6	6	6
7	7	7	7
8	8	8	8
9	9	9	9

CPE Paper 1 Reading Candidate Answer Sheet

Instructions

Use a PENCIL (B or HB). Mark ONE letter only for each question.
For example, if you think B is the right answer, mark your answer sheet like this:

0	A	B	C	D

Rub out any answer you wish to change using an eraser.

Part 1				
1	A	B	C	D
2	A	B	C	D
3	A	B	C	D
4	A	B	C	D
5	A	B	C	D
6	A	B	C	D
7	A	B	C	D
8	A	B	C	D
9	A	B	C	D
10	A	B	C	D
11	A	B	C	D
12	A	B	C	D
13	A	B	C	D
14	A	B	C	D
15	A	B	C	D
16	A	B	C	D
17	A	B	C	D
18	A	B	C	D

Part 2				
19	A	B	C	D
20	A	B	C	D
21	A	B	C	D
22	A	B	C	D
23	A	B	C	D
24	A	B	C	D
25	A	B	C	D
26	A	B	C	D

Part 3								
27	A	B	C	D	E	F	G	H
28	A	B	C	D	E	F	G	H
29	A	B	C	D	E	F	G	H
30	A	B	C	D	E	F	G	H
31	A	B	C	D	E	F	G	H
32	A	B	C	D	E	F	G	H
33	A	B	C	D	E	F	G	H

Part 4				
34	A	B	C	D
35	A	B	C	D
36	A	B	C	D
37	A	B	C	D
38	A	B	C	D
39	A	B	C	D
40	A	B	C	D

UNIVERSITY *of* CAMBRIDGE
ESOL Examinations

SAMPLE

Candidate Name
If not already printed, write name in CAPITALS and complete the Candidate No. grid (in pencil).

Candidate Signature

Examination Title

Centre

Supervisor:
If the candidate is ABSENT or has WITHDRAWN shade here

Centre No.

Candidate No.

Examination Details

0 0 0 0
1 1 1 1
2 2 2 2
3 3 3 3
4 4 4 4
5 5 5 5
6 6 6 6
7 7 7 7
8 8 8 8
9 9 9 9

CPE Paper 3 Use of English Candidate Answer Sheet 1

Instructions

Use a PENCIL (B or HB).

Rub out any answer you wish to change using an eraser.

For **Parts 1, 2** and **3**: Write your answer clearly in CAPITAL LETTERS. Write one letter in each box.

For example:

0 | M | A | Y

Answer **Parts 4 and 5** on Answer Sheet 2.

Write your answer neatly in the spaces provided.

You do not have to write in capital letters for Parts 4 and 5.

Part 1

Do not write below here

	Answer	Do not write below here
1		1 1 0
2		1 2 0
3		1 3 0
4		1 4 0
5		1 5 0
6		1 6 0
7		1 7 0
8		1 8 0
9		1 9 0
10		1 10 0
11		1 11 0
12		1 12 0
13		1 13 0
14		1 14 0
15		1 15 0

Part 2

Do not write below here

16		1 16 0
17		1 17 0
18		1 18 0
19		1 19 0
20		1 20 0
21		1 21 0
22		1 22 0
23		1 23 0
24		1 24 0
25		1 25 0

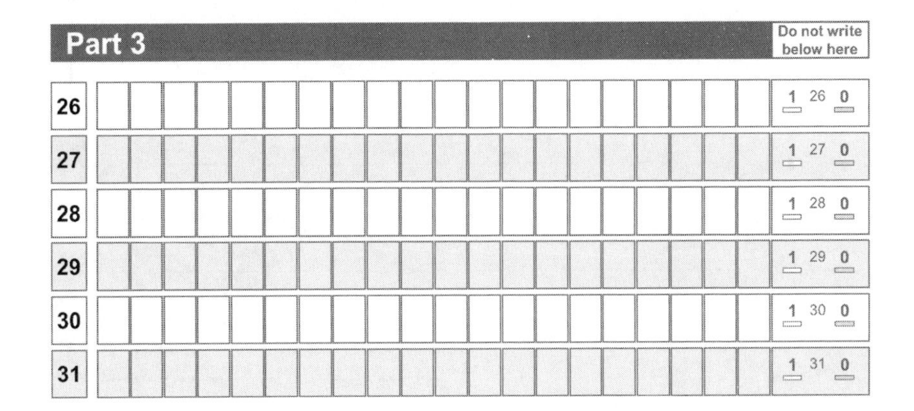

Part 3

Do not write below here

26		1 26 0
27		1 27 0
28		1 28 0
29		1 29 0
30		1 30 0
31		1 31 0

Continue with Parts 4 and 5 on Answer Sheet 2 ▶

UNIVERSITY *of* CAMBRIDGE
ESOL Examinations

SAMPLE

Candidate Name
If not already printed, write name in CAPITALS and complete the Candidate No. grid (in pencil).

Candidate Signature

Examination Title

Centre

Supervisor:
If the candidate is ABSENT or has WITHDRAWN shade here

Centre No.

Candidate No.

Examination Details

0	0	0	0
1	1	1	1
2	2	2	2
3	3	3	3
4	4	4	4
5	5	5	5
6	6	6	6
7	7	7	7
8	8	8	8
9	9	9	9

CPE Paper 3 Use of English Candidate Answer Sheet 2

Part 4

		Do not write below here
32		32 2 1 0
33		33 2 1 0
34		34 2 1 0
35		35 2 1 0
36		36 2 1 0
37		37 2 1 0
38		38 2 1 0
39		39 2 1 0

Part 5

Do not write below here

40		40 1 0
41		41 1 0
42		42 1 0
43		43 1 0

Part 5: question 44

For Examiner use only

Marks

Examiner number: Team and Position

Content	0	1	2	3	4

Language	0	1.1	1.2	2.1	2.2	3.1	3.2	4.1	4.2	5.1	5.2

0	0	0	0
1	1	1	1
2	2	2	2
3	3	3	3
4	4	4	4
5	5	5	5
6	6	6	6
7	7	7	7
8	8	8	8
9	9	9	9

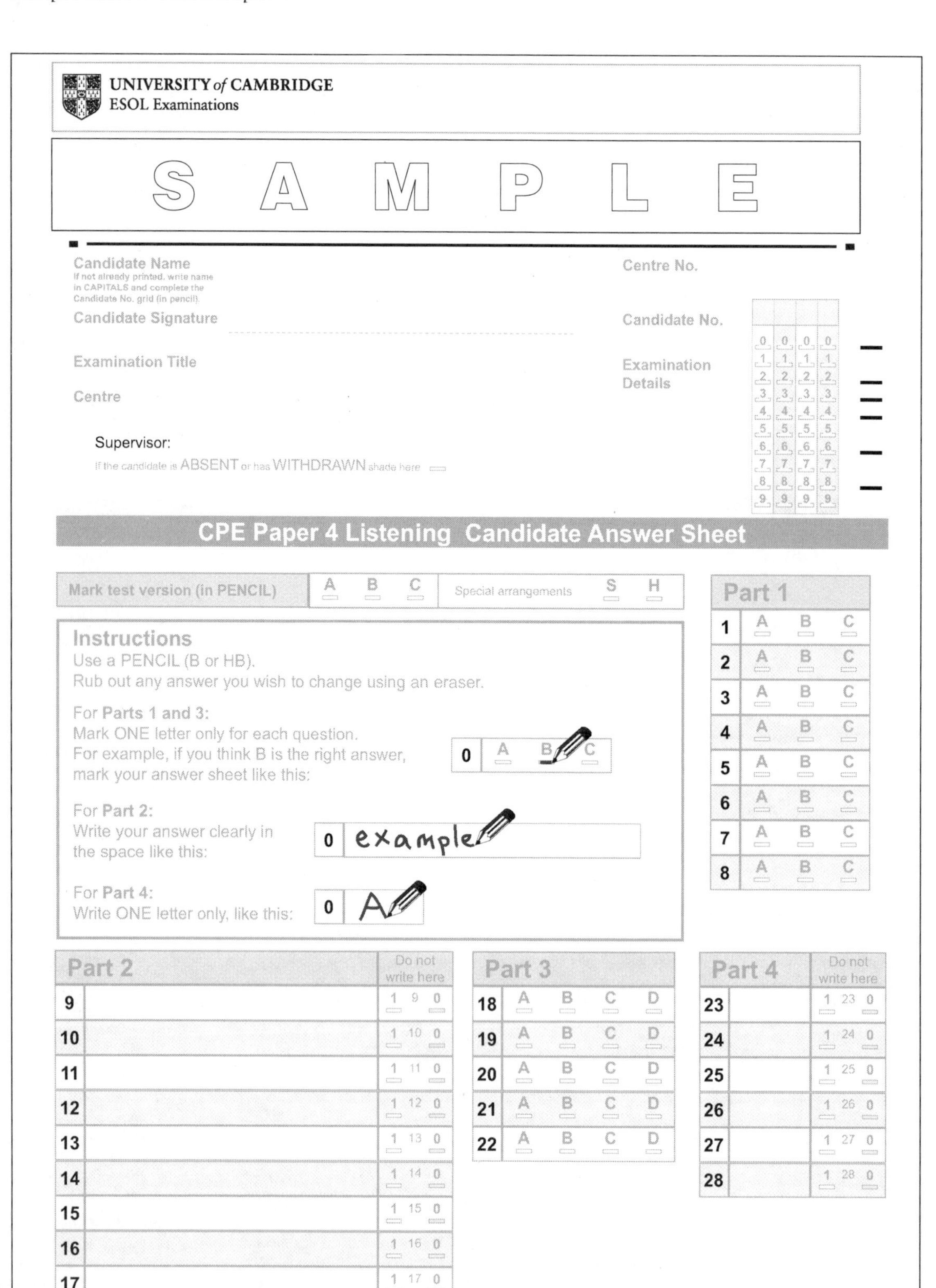

UNIVERSITY *of* CAMBRIDGE
ESOL Examinations

SAMPLE

Candidate Name
If not already printed, write name in CAPITALS and complete the Candidate No. grid (in pencil).

Centre No.

Candidate Signature

Candidate No.

Examination Title

Examination Details

Centre

Supervisor:
If the candidate is ABSENT or has WITHDRAWN shade here

CPE Paper 4 Listening Candidate Answer Sheet

Mark test version (in PENCIL) A B C | Special arrangements S H

Instructions
Use a PENCIL (B or HB).
Rub out any answer you wish to change using an eraser.

For **Parts 1 and 3:**
Mark ONE letter only for each question.
For example, if you think B is the right answer, mark your answer sheet like this:

0 A B C

For **Part 2:**
Write your answer clearly in the space like this:

0 example

For **Part 4:**
Write ONE letter only, like this:

0 A

Part 1			
1	A	B	C
2	A	B	C
3	A	B	C
4	A	B	C
5	A	B	C
6	A	B	C
7	A	B	C
8	A	B	C

Part 2		Do not write here
9		1 9 0
10		1 10 0
11		1 11 0
12		1 12 0
13		1 13 0
14		1 14 0
15		1 15 0
16		1 16 0
17		1 17 0

Part 3				
18	A	B	C	D
19	A	B	C	D
20	A	B	C	D
21	A	B	C	D
22	A	B	C	D

Part 4		Do not write here
23		1 23 0
24		1 24 0
25		1 25 0
26		1 26 0
27		1 27 0
28		1 28 0